THE GREAT
BOOK OF MEXICO

Interesting Stories, Mexican History,
& Random Facts About Mexico

History & Fun Facts

BILL O'NEILL

DON'T FORGET YOUR
FREE BOOKS

GET THEM FOR FREE ON
WWW.TRIVIABILL.COM

CONTENTS

CHAPTER FIVE

CHAPTER SIX
WEIRD MEXICO: FOLKLORE, LEGENDS,

INTRODUCTION

What do you really know about Mexico?

You probably know that Mexico touches America's southern border and that the people there speak Spanish. You probably also know that many of its coastal cities are popular tourist destinations, while dangerous cartels are common on the interior.

This book will explore such subjects, as well as others that pertain to "The United Mexican States." Yes, "Estados Unidos Mexicanos," which translates to "The United Mexican States," is the official name of Mexico because, like the United States of America, it is a collection of states under a federal government. We'll talk about that and so much more in this book, which is part history, part geography, part tour guide, and 100 percent fun!

You'll find that there is much more to North America's southern neighbor than you previously thought and that it is a country rich in history, culture, and folk customs. It is also an economic and cultural center for Latin America.

This book is broken up into six easy-to-follow chapters with fourteen to fifteen short stories in each that will help you learn more about Mexico. At the end of each chapter, we'll find out how much attention you've been paying by giving you some trivia questions to answer.

Some of the facts you'll read about are surprising. Some of them are weird. Some of them are cool. One thing they have in common is that they're all interesting! Once you've finished reading this book, you'll be guaranteed to walk away with more than you ever wanted to know about Mexico.

This book will answer the following questions:

How did Mexico get its name?

What is the deal with that snake on its flag?

Who were the first people to bring civilization and organized government to Mexico?

How did Mexico become a tourist and resort destination?

How did the cartels become so powerful?

What is Mexico's state-owned oil corporation?

What's the deal with those Mexican soap operas?

What are the two most popular sports in Mexico?

Why are female Mexican meteorologists so attractive?

And so much more!

CHAPTER ONE

MEXICO'S HISTORY BEFORE THE SPANISH

Centuries before Spanish became the predominant language of Mexico, the people of the land spoke a variety of different languages and belonged to different, yet related cultural groups. You probably know a little about some of these groups: the Olmecs, Mayans, and Aztecs. These peoples are among the best known, but there are others who were just as important. These lesser known peoples developed sophisticated governments, astronomical observatories, a writing system, and monumental temples.

Now what they did *on* those temples is something we'll get to in a little bit.

There is no way that we can talk about Mexican culture or Mexican history without talking about the pre-Columbian Period, which refers to any of the historical-cultural phases before the arrival of the

Spanish. Collectively, these pre-Columbian cultures are sometimes referred to as Mesoamerican Civilization because they are all located in central (meso) America. Modern Mexicans are proud of their pre-Columbian heritage and show it in a variety of ways. Their largest sports stadium is "Aztec Stadium," many pre-Columbian words are part of their lexicon, and some of the food their indigenous ancestors ate is part of the modern Mexican diet.

So let's take a look at these fascinating pre-Columbian peoples and the role they played in shaping Mexican history.

The Rubber People

Have you ever heard the term "Rubber People" in reference to ancient Mexico?

Probably not, because the most common name used to refer to the first advanced people is "Olmec," which is actually derived from the Aztec word meaning "rubber people." Unfortunately, since Olmec writing has only recently been discovered and scholars don't yet understand it, we don't know what the Olmecs called themselves. Because of this, we use the Aztec designation. We'll get to the Aztecs a bit later, but for now let's talk about the Olmecs and how they got that strange name.

Well, the Olmecs were so named because they came

from the region of southeast Mexico on the coast of the Gulf of Mexico that is known for its rubber trees. Rubber played an important role in many of the pre-Columbian Mexican cultures because these peoples used to make balls for their sacred "Ball Game," which the Olmecs invented.

In fact, the Olmecs were the first Mesoamericans to do and invent a lot of things.

After the Olmec culture formed around 1200 BC, the people began to congregate and eventually urbanize near what is the modern city of La Venta. It was at La Venta where the first Mesoamerican pyramid was built, the first blood rituals took place (which included the Ball Game), and the earliest calendrical observations were made.

In fact, the Olmecs were the first people of Mexico to develop a "long count calendar" and the concept of zero, both of which were utilized by later peoples in pre-Columbian Mexico.

Recent research has also revealed that the Olmecs were the first people of Mexico to develop writing, hundreds of years earlier than what was previously believed. As we will see, many of the Olmecs' ideas were later adopted and sometimes improved upon by later Mesoamerican peoples, such as the Mayans and Aztecs.

Truly, the Olmecs were an incredible and often

overlooked people who made an incredible contribution to the history of Mexico and the world!

Your People Call It Corn

Corn is a big part of the modern American diet. Canned and frozen corn are bought and consumed throughout the year and during the summer; it is also common to see farmers selling their "sweet corn" from the back of pickup trucks in parking lots. And of course, "feed corn" is what is used to feed most of the cows, chickens, and pigs we eat every year.

But the word corn is actually not accurate.

Before the Spanish colonized the Americas, "corn" referred generically to just about any grain: barley, flax, wheat, etc. In fact, in many places around the world the term corn is still used to refer to most grains. What we modern Americans refer to as corn, though, is actually "maize."

The word maize comes from a Spanish word, which was taken from a Taino Indian word for the crop. Although the Taino speaking peoples lived in the Caribbean Islands, maize domestication began in Mexico near the Olmecs' homeland.

In order for the Olmecs to transition into civilization status, they needed to go through the period where they domesticated agriculture the way the people in Egypt and the Fertile Crescent did a couple of thousand years earlier. Although the people of Mexico had few animals to domesticate and none of them were large, they did have an abundance of wild maize.

By 2500 BC domestic maize varieties had spread throughout Mexico, and about one thousand years after that the first signs of true civilization cropped up in Mesoamerica in the form of the Olmecs. Maize played a key role in the Olmec diet and along with basalt, which was used by various Mesoamerican peoples to build monuments, was a central commodity in their trade.

As we will see a little later, maize was a focal point in many Mesoamerican religions and was the primary ingredient used to make tacos, tortillas, and burritos.

So if there is one food that you could say "made" Mexico, it would be what the Mesoamericans called maize and what we call corn.

What's with Those Big Heads

Even if you knew little to nothing about the Olmecs before reading this, chances are you've seen images of the colossal heads they created. The Olmecs used the basalt of their region to carve these large heads, ranging from four to twelve feet high, which are believed to be of their rulers. The (presumably male) figures are notable for their features: squinted eyes, flat noses, and a cap or helmet on the head. Scholars point out that modern people from the region bear a resemblance to the figures, and they surmise the cap/helmet may have been associated with the ball game.

Most of the heads are dated before 1000 BC, although the largest ones from Tres Zapotes and La Cabota are dated to around 900 BC.

The basalt needed for the statues was mined from the mountains near Veracruz and then brought to workshops where sculptors chipped away at the blocks until they achieved a likeness of the ruler. The backs of the statues are flat, which would have saved the sculptors time and made the process a bit easier.

Although the heads demonstrate that the Olmecs were capable of great craftsmanship, perhaps the true marvel of these creations is in the organization of the labor. The basalt boulders had to be transported about ninety miles from the quarry to the workshops, which would have required a fair amount of manpower. To make matters more difficult, the Olmecs didn't have knowledge of the wheel.

So how did the Olmecs move these blocks, some of which weighed more than fifty tons? Modern scholars believe that the Olmecs took advantage of the many rivers and streams in the region to move these blocks, and when none were available they used their muscles to drag them.

It may not have been the easiest way to do things, but it worked for the Olmecs and also provided a template for later Mesoamerican peoples.

Before It Was Called Mexico City

If you've ever been to some of the small villages of rural Mexico and then traveled to Mexico City you were probably overcome with the latter's hustle and bustle. It is, after all, Mexico's capital and largest city and one of the largest cities in the world. The freeways above and the subway below move millions of people around the metropolitan area daily.

But in ancient times the area around Mexico City was also full of life.

Sure they didn't have cars, subways, or airplanes, but hundreds of thousands of people congregated in the area to create Mexico's first true urban area.

After the decline of the Olmec culture, the focus of Mesoamerican civilization shifted south to the Mayan lands (we'll get to them in a little bit) and north to the Central Mexican Valley, which is also known as the "Valley of Mexico." The valley is located on a plateau, has a minimum elevation of seven thousand feet, and is surrounded by mountains. In the middle of the Central Mexican Valley, in ancient times, was Lake Texcoco, which provided the people of the valley with a source of food, water, and transportation.

Just northeast of modern Mexico City, and located a few miles east of Lake Texcoco, was the sleepy market town of Teotihuacán. Teotihuacán grew from a small village in 200 BC to a city of about forty thousand people by AD 100. It is believed that Teotihuacán's growth was the result of it being a major religious center in the Central Mexican Valley—people from the other towns in the valley came there for religious rituals and festivals.

And the city would've been quite impressive.

In fact, if you're ever in Mexico City, be sure to make the short trip to Teotihuacán to see its many extraordinary pyramid temples. The Pyramids of the Sun and Moon are the two most impressive of the temples, as they dominate the landscape; from a distance, they seem to blend in with the mountains.

The Pyramid of the Sun was completed sometime in the AD 100s and is the third biggest pyramid in the world with a height of two hundred sixteen feet, a width of seven hundred sixty feet, and a length of seven hundred twenty feet.

Teotihuacán came to rule the entire Central Mexican Valley, which today would be the area of modern Mexico City, until it was destroyed around AD 700. But civilization, as we will see later, continued to thrive in the region.

The Emergence of the Mayans

The next major Mesoamerican cultural group to emerge in ancient Mexico, and perhaps the most important, was the Mayans. The Mayan people began to form as a distinct ethnic group around 400 BC in the rain forests of what is today Guatemala and the Yucatan Peninsula of Mexico. The Mayans were an agricultural people, growing maize and tree crops such as cacao and avocado. By AD 200 the Mayans had developed a sophisticated culture that used writing, made advanced astronomical observations, and built some of the finest cities in the pre-Columbian Americas.

Because of that, the era of Mayan dominance, which lasted until around AD 900, is often called the Classical Period of Mesoamerican history.

The Mayans took many of the ideas and inventions of the Olmecs and improved them; these were then later utilized by other people in the region such as the Aztecs. The cultural sophistication of the Mayans is incredible, especially when you consider that they never had a central government or unified state—there was no "Mayan Empire."

So now you're probably wondering, what did the Mayans have for a government?

Well, the Mayans were divided into independent city-states, similar to ancient Greece, but with a very different type of government system. The Mayan cities were monarchies ruled by dynasties, with a heavy influence from the priesthood. Their form of government was similar to those in ancient Mesopotamia, ancient Egypt, and other Bronze Age cultures.

Some of the largest and most important Mayan city-states were Tikal, Chichen Itza, and Copan, though there were hundreds of independent cities and thousands altogether.

But they were not all friends.

In fact, the Mayans were very warlike people and regularly conducted major military campaigns against rival city-states for resources such as obsidian, jade, and perhaps most importantly — prisoners for human sacrifice rituals! Yes, human sacrifice and "blood rituals" in general played a very important role in Mayan religion and culture.

You can't properly understand pre-Columbian Mexico without understanding how and why these people conducted blood rituals.

Blood for the Gods

In order to understand Mexico's pre-Columbian history, you need to know that blood played a major role, especially the shedding of it. These so-called blood rituals were first recorded by the Olmecs, and then turned into a science by the Mayans. The need to shed blood came from the Mayan religion.

Like most pre-modern peoples, the Mayans were polytheistic, having a pantheon of more than one hundred sixty-six deities. They had storm gods, fertility goddesses, and war gods. But one of the most important was Hun Ixim, the maize god.

According to the Mayan creation myth, Hun Ixim made humans from corn and water and to thank him blood needed to be shed regularly. Mayans from all strata of society would take part in a variety of different bloodletting rituals, the most important of which were done by the nobles.

And they were no doubt quite painful!

Women would cut a hole in their lip with an obsidian blade, run a string through the hole, and let the blood collect on a thin piece of bark. After the bark collected enough blood, a prayer would be said and the bark would be burned. The first few times probably would have been the most painful, but after awhile chances are the lips would lose much of their feeling.

As agonizing as that may have been, it would have been worse for the noble males.

The men would also use a string, but instead of running it through their lip they would place it through a hole they cut in the foreskin of their penis.

Ouch!

Remember this was to appease their gods, so any amount of pain would have been temporary compared to the eternal rewards, right?

Offering their own blood was not the only way the Mayans shed blood for their gods. Human sacrifice was a pretty common thing and was conducted on or near their pyramid temples. Since the Mayans were usually at war with each other, there was no shortage of sacrifice victims either. War captives were regularly sacrificed for the attainment of good crops, for religious festivals, and for recently deceased nobles. Usually, rival warriors were the victims. But that didn't mean others were safe from harm. In AD 738, the king of Copán was captured and sacrificed by a rival city.

It wasn't necessarily all blood and gore in the Mayan cities though, there were plenty of other things taking place as well.

Pyramids Everywhere

One of the things that most people immediately notice about pre-Columbian Mexico is that there are pyramids all over the place. We've already discussed how the Olmecs built the first pyramid in Mexico and then more (larger ones) were later built at Teotihuacán. But the Mayans built more pyramids—and by all accounts nicer looking ones—than any other Mesoamerican people.

The Mayan pyramids may not have been as large as the other pyramids, but they were constructed better.

The most impressive and most visited of all the Mayan pyramids is known as "El Castillo" in Chichen Itza.

El Castillo is a limestone step pyramid that stands ninety-eight feet tall with the temple on its summit. The base is one hundred eighty-one feet across, which makes it considerably smaller than the Pyramid of the Sun at Teotihuacán, but it has much more detail—sculptures of the feathered serpent god Kukulkan are located at different places on the pyramid.

So, as we talk about the Mayan pyramids and those built by earlier peoples in pre-Columbian Mexico, you may be wondering: was there a connection between the ancient Egyptians and people of ancient Mexico?

The answer is, most certainly, no.

Once you get past the superficial fact that Mesoamerican pyramids and Egyptian pyramids had a similar shape, you quickly find many more differences. The Egyptian pyramids were built more than two thousand years before the Mexican pyramids and served very different purposes. The Egyptian pyramids were used exclusively as tombs for the kings and their wives. The Mesoamerican pyramids, however, were primarily used as temples: human sacrifice rituals often took place on top the pyramids.

The reason for the similarity in shape is unknown, but many scholars believe it had to do with the limited technology both groups possessed—it is easier to build a mound-type structure than a more elaborate temple as the Egyptians did later in their history.

The triangular shape may also have to do with the fact that both the Egyptians and the peoples of Mesoamerica worshipped the sun. The pyramids could have represented the rays of the sun giving life to the Egyptian pharaohs in their tombs or, in Mesoamerica, taking life from the sacrifice victims.

Whatever the reason, there was no ancient connection between the two civilizations.

The End of the World

Remember a few years ago when people were saying that the Mayans predicted the end of the world would happen in 2012? It was all over the Internet and a movie was even kind of made about it. Then when 2012 came and went without a major apocalypse people quickly forgot about it all.

But what was that "prediction" based on?

Most of the people of Mesoamerica were very good astronomers and mathematicians and so they were able to develop pretty accurate calendars. All of the different Mesoamerican peoples used versions of the same calendar, which is known as the "Long Count Calendar," but the Mayans developed the most accurate of all the calendars, devising a 365-day year.

The Long Count was subdivided into shorter cycles. A good way to visualize this is as a big wheel moving forward (the Long Count), with smaller wheels within it also moving (the shorter cycles). According to the Gregorian Calendar (the calendar of the modern world), December 20, 2012 was the end of another cycle. The Mayans were a literate people and left inscriptions with some of their calendrical observations, but none mention any chaos associated with the end of the cycle.

I guess we'll just have to wait three hundred eighty-seven years for the next cycle to end!

Play Ball!

Today, spectator sports are an important part of people's pastimes in nearly every country in the world. Whether it is football/soccer in Europe, most of Latin America, Africa, and the Middle East, or baseball in North America and parts of Latin America and Asia, most of us love to watch, follow, and sometimes bet on our favorite sports.

The people of Mesoamerica were no different, but with one major exception.

The losers in their favorite sport lost not only the match, but usually their lives!

The "ball game," as it is called in English, was known by a number of different names to the various Mesoamerican peoples. We aren't quite sure about the specific rules. However, based on a game played in Central America today and extant ball courts, scholars believe that it was played by two teams of varying sizes with the objective being to either keep the ball in play or hit it through a hoop type goal. The ball was made of solid rubber, weighing up to ten pounds, and would be moved by players hitting it with their hips.

As mentioned earlier, the Olmecs were the first people in Mexico to play the ball game, probably around the time they became a sophisticated society in 1200 BC.

The ball courts were long rectangles with sloped sidewalls, often in an "I" shape, but there was no standard size. One of the best preserved ball courts is at the Mayan city of Chichen Itza, which is dug several feet into the ground. On the ground level is a stone ring on each side; these are believed to have been the goals.

It is believed that the ball games were public sporting events (at least for the nobles and elites) and that, like most other elements of Mesoamerican culture, they had religious significance. Some scholars also think that ball games occasionally served as a substitute for warfare and that the Mayans used them as an elaborate way to conduct human sacrifice rituals. Inscriptions on the wall of the ball court at Chichen Itza show a decapitated ballplayer with snakes coming from where his head was previously. This, and other Mayan inscriptions, has led modern scholars to think that the losers were sacrificed.

Not only were the losers sacrificed, but it is believed that their heads may have been used as balls!

Back to the Valley

The Mayan culture never truly collapsed. They were still living in some of their cities when the Spanish arrived, and there is still a distinct Mayan culture in southern Mexico today. With that said, by about AD 900 the Mayan influence over Mexico had severely waned and the power in the region had shifted back north to the Central Mexican Valley.

The city of Tula, just north of Lake Texcoco, became the capital of the group known as the Toltecs. The Toltecs carried on many of the traditions of their Mesoamerican predecessors, eventually building an empire that encompassed most of Mexico and lasted from about AD 968 to AD 1168. The Toltecs even conquered some of the more prominent Mayan sites, such as Chichen Itza, and added their own personality to the existing monuments.

The primary god of the Toltecs was Quetzalcoatl, a feathered serpent, which was similar to the Mayan Kukulkan.

The idea of human sacrifice became much more institutionalized under the Toltecs and was done on a much more industrial scale. The Toltecs began conducting longer and more extensive military campaigns in order to acquire more land and resources. Basalt, jade, and hematite from southern Mexico and obsidian from all throughout the region flowed into Tula, making the city and its nobles very wealthy. Of course, captives for human sacrifice rituals were also brought to the city.

But as the Toltecs got fat off the land, they ignored an impending threat from the north that was about to bring their empire down.

Looking for a Home

As the Toltecs' carefully constructed empire collapsed, the final and perhaps most important people was about to enter the Central Mexican Valley—the Aztecs.

The Aztecs' early history is shrouded in mystery because they didn't have writing and also because their oral history blurred the line between historical fact and myth. To add to this confusion, the naming of the Aztecs is also a bit confusing. Anthropologists and historians have been able to reconstruct their journey somewhat accurately, though.

The Aztecs originated somewhere in what would today be the southwest United States, in a semi-mythical place they called Aztlan, which is where the term "Aztec" originated. The Aztecs, though, were members of the "Mexica" tribe, which is how they referred to themselves. As you can guess, this is where the modern name of Mexico is derived. Not to confuse you any more, but the Aztec language was known as "Nahuatl."

You're probably wondering, "If the Aztecs were from the American southwest, how did they end up in what is today Mexico City?"

Well, the southwest in the 1100s was much like it is today: dry, inhospitable, and unable to support large populations without advanced technology.

So the Mexica began a migration southward, fighting other people along the way. Their movements pushed other people south in a domino effect, which contributed to the collapse of the Toltec Empire. The Mexica/Aztecs finally arrived in the Central Mexican Valley around 1300 but were not welcomed with open arms. The sedentary and civilized people of the valley viewed the bellicose semi-nomadic people as both outsiders and barbarians.

But they were barbarians that could be useful.

The Eagle and the Cactus

Although the Aztecs were brave and formidable warriors, they were not very organized. As a result, they were routinely defeated and somewhat bullied by the urbanized peoples of the Central Mexican Valley. This continued until the king of the city of Culhuacan saw that the warrior Aztecs could be useful. He gave them what was believed to be some worthless land and allowed them to have one of his sons so they could start a royal line.

But the different customs of the Mexica quickly became a problem.

The people of Culhuacan and the other city-states in the valley may have practiced human sacrifice, but they had their limits. So when the Mexica sacrificed a Culhuacan princess and turned her skin into an elaborate ritual costume, it did not sit well with her father, to say the least.

The Aztecs were once more on the run.

They fled to a swampy area of Lake Texcoco. Then, according to Aztec legend, in 1325 one of the leaders had a vision of an eagle perched on a cactus eating a snake. The vision was a sign for the Mexica to build their city right there in the *middle* of the lake.

The industrious Aztecs piled bucket after bucket of earth into the lake until they finally had enough land for a settlement. The settlement quickly grew into a large city that became, Tenochtitlan, the capital and nerve center of the Aztec Empire.

And the vision that brought them there would later serve as Mexico's coat of arms and would become the center piece of the flag of Mexico.

I Heart Huitzilopochtli

As the Aztecs were building Tenochtitlan, they were also establishing a royal dynasty and an alliance that would first rule over the Central Mexican Valley and then most of Mexico. Under King Itzcoatl (who ruled from 1427-1440), the Aztecs formed an alliance with the cities of Texcoco and Tlacopan, making them the preeminent military, economic, and cultural power in the valley. Wars of conquest soon followed, which brought jade, obsidian, limestone, and jaguar pelts into the city.

It also brought plenty of captives for human sacrifice.

Like all of the other peoples of Mesoamerica before them, the Aztecs performed human sacrifice, but they did so on a much greater scale, even more so than the Mayans. The primary Aztec god was the warrior god, Huitzilopochtli, who demanded a steady supply of human hearts.

The Aztecs were only too willing to appease him!

Warriors from the lowest rungs on the social ladder were allowed to advance to all but the highest positions if they captured enough live warriors for sacrifice rituals. The Aztec leaders would even set up prearranged battles called "Flower Wars" for the warriors to take more captives. The outcomes of the Flower Wars were never in doubt—the Aztecs were always victorious—but it was a competition to capture the most men.

The Aztecs also conducted elaborate celebrations when they won major battles, such as in 1475 when they defeated the last of the other Mexica tribes. In order to give proper thanks to Huitzilopochtli, the Aztecs sacrificed twenty thousand people in one month.

That's a lot of hearts!

Floating Gardens and Causeways

In addition to being industrious, the Aztecs were great innovators of existing Mesoamerican technologies and ideas. The Aztecs continued to use the calendars of their predecessors and they also played the ball game. More importantly, however, they devised ways that allowed their city to grow despite being in the middle of a lake.

The Aztecs built a number of causeways that radiated out from Tenochtitlan to the other cities in their alliance. The causeways allowed trade to flow and also enabled the quick transport of their warriors, who didn't have the luxury of horses to carry them long distances.

But you may be wondering: "Since the Aztecs lived on a man-made island, where did they get most of their food?"

Of course, some of their food came from people they conquered throughout Mexico, but they were able to grow most of their maize for local consumption through an ingenious invention known as a *chinampa*. The Aztec word chinampa is often translated into "floating garden" because it is a plot of crops that appears to float on water.

These floating gardens were made by weaving reeds together with stakes, which created a small, man-made island that appeared to float. Crops of all types could then be planted and farmed on these floating gardens. Floating gardens provided most of the agricultural needs for the Aztecs and became such an important part of their culture that they survived the arrival of the Spanish.

Floating gardens are still in use in some parts of Mexico around Mexico City.

The Return of Quetzalcoatl?

The year 1519 proved to be a major turning point in Mexico's history. That was the year when Spanish conquistador Hernan Cortés and about three thousand of his men landed on the shores of Mexico near the modern town of Veracruz. This moment began the period of extended "first contact" between Europeans and indigenous peoples that would continue for decades.

But for the Aztecs it was all over by August of 1521.

In the years before the Spanish arrival in Mexico, the Aztec King Montezuma II (1466-1520) is said to have been told about many bad omens. According to the Aztec calendar, 1519 was also the beginning of a new cycle where the god Quetzalcoatl was supposed to return to Mexico. Though many of the Spanish sources claim that Montezuma believed that Cortés was the ancient god, a number of modern scholars remain skeptical about this.

Regardless of whether Montezuma believed Cortés was a god or not, the Spanish certainly made an impression on the people of Mesoamerica. Their horses looked like "big dogs," their armor was mysterious, and their guns and cannons seemed to be from another world. Their appearance was also otherworldly: their skin was white, some of their hair was golden or the color of blood, and some had eyes that were blue or green.

Once Cortés learned of the Aztec Empire and its wealth from emissaries sent by Montezuma, he set his sights on conquering it. He made alliances with enemies of the Aztecs, such as Tlaxcala, and then marched to Tenochtitlan, which in 1519 was larger than any city in Spain. When the Spanish arrived they were greeted kindly by Montezuma, who proceeded to basically give the empire to Cortés.

The Aztec nobles, seeing that the Spanish weren't gods, drove the outsiders from the main temple and the city itself. But Cortés later returned with his men and Tlaxcala allies, laid siege to Tenochtitlan, and reattacked the city, destroying the Aztec Empire in the process.

The surprise attack did not make their victory a foregone conclusion, but the Spanish had many advantages in their favor. The advanced weaponry and armor certainly gave them an advantage and, although they were vastly outnumbered to begin with, the Tlaxcalans gave their army a much needed boost in numbers and intelligence. There was also the fact that Aztecs fought battles to take live captives, rarely to kill.

Though wars between the Spanish and indigenous people continued in Mexico until the end of the century, the destruction of the Aztec Empire generally marks the end of Mexico's pre-Columbian history and the beginning of its modern period.

RANDOM FACTS

1. Although the level of development of the Mesoamerican cultures is often considered to be Bronze Age, none of the people developed bronze or any other major metals for use. For knives, spear points, and other sharp and pointed weapons, the Mesoamericans used the volcanic rock obsidian. Obsidian can be easily worked by chipping it to make sharp and pointed edges.

2. Although the Mayan "classic period" ended around 900 when the city-states in the central area collapsed, Mayan culture continued on the Yucatan. The Mayans were still around when Cortés showed up 1500s.

3. The Aztecs were able to gain control over the Central Mexican Valley by forming an alliance with the cities of Tetzcoco and Tlocopan in the 1420s, which is today referred to as the "Triple Alliance."

4. Cortés was able to communicate with his Indian allies through a translator, Gerónimo de Aguilar. Aguilar was a Franciscan friar who was shipwrecked on the Yucatan and captured by a Mayan chief. Aguilar, along with another

Spaniard named Gonzalo Guerrero, escaped and found refuge in another Mayan city-state, where Aguilar was a slave but Guerrero became a convert to the Mayan religion and a warrior. Aguilar later joined Cortés and he used his knowledge of Mayan to communicate with an Indian woman named La Malinche, who knew Mayan and Aztec. The two served as the primary translators during the Conquest of Mexico.

5. Many of the weapons the Mayans and Aztecs used in battle are considered nonlethal. Clubs and lassos were common; these were used to capture people live so they could later be used as sacrifice victims.

6. The Great Pyramid of Cholula, in Cholula, Mexico, is the largest pyramid in Mexico. Although it isn't quite as tall as the Pyramid of the Sun in Teotihuacan, it covers a greater land area. A Catholic church sits on the pyramid's summit today.

7. Cortés' mission was initially unsanctioned, as the governor of Cuba wanted to replace him before he left. The initial force only consisted of about six hundred men, but more came from Cuba later.

8. In order to ensure loyalty and to guarantee that none of his men would think about mutiny and

returning to Cuba, Cortés destroyed all of the ships they had arrived in. This move probably helped galvanize the Spanish, making them an even more formidable fighting force.

9. There were no major pack animals in pre-Columbian Mexico. In fact, the only pack animals in all of the Americas before the Spanish were alpacas and llamas, but those were thousands of miles to the south in the Andes. The lack of large domestic animals impacted the diet of Mesoamericans. They did consume deer, peccary, and dogs; but their main sources of protein were from beans and legumes.

10. Jade was a prized mineral among all the Mesoamerican peoples for cosmetic reasons. Jade was used to make ornate necklaces, earrings, and body piercings.

11. Experts subdivide Olmec history into three subphases: Early Formative (1800-900 BC), Middle Formative (900-400 BC), and Late Formative (400 BC-AD 200). Most of La Venta was built during the Middle Formative period, which is also when most of the Olmec heads were built.

12. Since the Olmec heads are not accompanied by any written texts, they have been the subject of speculation by nonexperts. Some of the theories

about the origins of the heads are bizarre and not based on any real facts. Some say the Olmec heads are proof of Atlantis or aliens, and others say they resemble Africans. Scholars have proven that the statues were carved with local materials and existing technologies, and that they indeed resemble the local population.

13. None of the Mesoamerican peoples constructed "ships" in the conventional sense of the word. They did, however, build and use canoes, which the Aztecs used in a lake battle against the Spanish.

14. Many of the Mesoamerican peoples employed some basic writing, but only the Mayans had a complete alphabet and writing system. Their writing is often compared to Egyptian hieroglyphs, but as with the pyramids, it is only a matter of coincidence. Beyond the superficial similarities the two languages are quite different. Their language didn't become accurately deciphered until after World War II, and even today scholars are still refining their understanding of Mayan.

15. After conquering Mexico, Cortés explored and conquered many more places in the Americas. He eventually returned to Spain and led military expeditions against the Ottoman Empire. He planned to return to Mexico in 1547 but died in

Spain, in debt and the defendant in many lawsuits. His image in modern Mexico is somewhat mixed: although he is not necessarily disparaged as a villain, he is also rarely viewed as a national hero.

16. If an Aztec commoner committed twenty heroic deeds on the battlefield, he could wear cotton and sandals, enter and dine in the royal palace, and could join the elite Eagle and Jaguar Corps.

17. Pulque was a popular Aztec alcoholic drink. It was made from the fermented sap of the maguey plant and had a whitish color. Pulque was viewed as a spiritual drug by the Aztecs and, as such, only the nobles and priest class were allowed to drink it. Warriors who did twenty heroic acts were also allowed to drink pulque.

18. The Mesoamerican ball game's modern descendant is known as "ulama." Ulama is played in the Mexican state of Sinaloa and is popular with members of the Indian community. Thankfully, the losers of today's ball game are not sacrificed to the gods.

19. Those skeptical of the idea that Montezuma believed that Cortés was Quetzalcoatl, think that the Aztec king allowed the Spanish to enter Tenochtitlan in order to learn more about them before making a move. Once inside the city, though, Cortés made Montezuma his captive.

20. The type of gun that the Spanish used against the Aztecs was called an arquebus. An arquebus was a pre-musket long gun that was often mounted on a post when fired for stability. Cortés also brought with him several crossbowmen, who used a type of crossbow that shot bolts that could easily penetrate Aztec cotton armor.

Test Yourself – Questions

1. Which of these was the first advanced Mesoamerican culture?

   a. Toltec
   b. Olmec
   c. Aztec

2. Which of these people lived in southern Mexico?

   a. Aztecs
   b. Mayans
   c. Zapotecs

3. This volcanic rock was used to make weapons in ancient Mexico:

   a. Basalt
   b. Jade
   c. Obsidian

4. He was the feathered serpent god popular in central Mexico:

   a. Quetzalcoatl
   b. Zeus
   c. Corn God

5. The modern Mexican flag is partly inspired from which of these people?

   a. Aztecs
   b. Mayans
   c. Olmecs

Answers

1. b
2. b
3. c
4. a
5. a

CHAPTER TWO

MEXICO'S HISTORY AFTER THE ARRIVAL OF THE SPANISH

What do you know about Mexico's history after the arrival of the Spanish? Did you know that Mexico was part of a larger colony for nearly three hundred years and that its rebellion—once it broke out—was partly inspired by the American Revolution? Did you know that the French briefly occupied Mexico in the mid-1800s, and when they were finally driven out it became a major holiday celebrated in Mexico and elsewhere? Keep reading to find out how Mexico developed as an independent country and learn about some of the ups and downs its people have experienced.

The Colony of New Spain

After the Spanish conquered Mexico in 1521, they had to organize their newly won territory in an efficient way. The problem was it was such a vast territory. Not only did the Spanish conquer what is today Mexico, but they also ruled the areas that are today the American states west of the Mississippi River, in addition to Florida, as well as most of Central and South America. In fact, it would probably be easier to consider what the Spanish *didn't* rule in the Americas in the 1500s.

The French had what is today Quebec and some Caribbean Islands, while the British and Dutch had what is today the east coast of the United States and some Caribbean Islands. The Portuguese controlled what is now Brazil.

With such a vast under their command, the Spanish divided their American colonies into four districts known as viceroyalties: the Viceroyalty of New Granada, the Viceroyalty of the Rio de la Plata, the Viceroyalty of Peru, and the Viceroyalty of New Spain, which represented Mexico, Central America, most of the Caribbean, and all Spanish possessions north of the Rio Grande.

The Viceroyalty of New Spain was officially created in 1535 with its capital in Ciudad de Mexico, or Mexico City. New Spain became attractive to Spanish settlers almost immediately for a number of reasons. Silver and lead were discovered in the mountains near Zacatecas in the 1540s, which brought a flood of Spanish investors.

But Spanish merchants and nobles weren't about to do the dirty and dangerous work in the mines. Lucky for them, Mexico had one of the highest indigenous populations in all of the Spanish colonies. The Indians were put to work in the mines, often forcibly, bringing a huge surplus of silver into Spain and eventually Europe.

Those with business interests were not the only ones who liked to exploit the large Indian population of Mexico; Christian missionaries were also guilty of this. They went to jungle villages and isolated mountain communities to bring the word of God to the former Mayan and Aztec peoples.

New Spain quickly became an important part of the Spanish Empire, even before it was fully explored.

The Seven Cities of Gold

When New Spain was incorporated into the Spanish Empire, brave men were needed to explore its vast reaches. Many of these men came to Mexico looking for a fresh start; others were in search of gold.

Yes, legends of cities literally paved with gold became quite common among the Spanish in the

1500s and 1600s. No doubt you've heard at least a little about some of these legends, such as the lost city of El Dorado, right? Well, one of the most important ones in Mexico's history was the legend of the Seven Cities of Gold, known collectively as Cibola.

When a Spanish noble named Francisco Vázquez de Coronado y Luján (usually referred to as "Coronado") first heard about Cibola, he decided that he would be the one to find the cities of gold.

As was common with many young Spanish men of his generation who were born into a noble family, Coronado traveled to Mexico in 1535 at the age of twenty-five to make a fortune and a name for himself. Coronado married and settled in Mexico City, but his restless spirit soon got the best of him when he heard about Cibola.

Coronado decided he would be the man to find the fabled Seven Cities of Gold.

After raising the necessary funds and compiling a force of several hundred Europeans and more than two thousand Indians, Coronado led his expedition out of Compostela on February 23, 1540. He guided them north along what is known as the Sinaloa Coast.

After several months of travel, Coronado and his men eventually ended up in what is today the American southwest, where they attacked and killed many Pueblo Indians, but didn't find any cities of gold. Coronado, then hearing that the cities were even farther north than he initially believed, led his men into what is today Kansas. Coronado finally put an end to the expedition after about two years and returned to Mexico City.

Although Coronado never found the cities of gold, he left his name throughout the American southwest as well as plenty of money and land for his family in Mexico, where he died in 1554.

Rewards for Conquest

In order to understand Mexico's early modern history, it is important to know that early modern Spain was a fairly warlike society. In 1492, besides discovering the Americas, the Spanish also drove the Muslim Moors—who had ruled the country for hundreds of years—out of Spain. Most of the Spanish men who came to New Spain in the early 1500s were veterans of fighting the Moors, as well as their occasional European neighbors. So they were often fairly violent and always looking for plunder.

These were the men from whom the term *conquistador* originated.

The Spanish crown knew that colonizing the Americas wouldn't be easy, so they decided to use the existing *encomienda* system as an enticement.

Under the encomienda system, Spanish conquistadors who took land from the Muslims in Spain were given land to farm and a set number of Muslims from villages on that land to work as labor.

Yes, it was a form of slavery, but it wasn't chattel slavery. The land owners didn't own any individuals, though they did have control over the labor of a specific group.

When the Spanish first began settling New Spain, they used the encomienda system to exploit the labor of the indigenous peoples. Since there were so many Indian groups in Mexico and Central America, the conquistadors had a large labor pool ready to farm their encomiendas.

And most conquistadors were willing to work their Indian labor to death to turn a small profit. Although the encomienda system was not originally intended to be a form of chattel slavery, it quickly devolved into that by the 1520s—Indian workers had no rights and couldn't leave the land. To make matters worse, the Spanish inadvertently brought diseases with them, such as small pox, against which the Indians had little immunity.

Unable to ignore the problems with the cruel encomienda system, the Spanish Crown finally ended it in 1542.

A New Social Caste System Was Born

The social and cultural development of New Spain played a major role in the type of culture that Mexico was to become. Since New Spain was a Spanish colony, it relied on Spanish laws for the most part. However, it also developed many of its own laws.

Among some of the laws of New Spain were ones that discouraged racial miscegenation, or mixing.

Now this didn't stop mixing from happening, especially since most of the Europeans who immigrated to Mexico were single men. Many of these early conquistadors took Indian women as wives or mistresses and in the process created a new class of people known as *mestizos*. Technically speaking, a mestizo is person who is half Indian and half white/European. Today, mestizos comprise the majority of the population of Mexico, but in early New Spain they were just one of four major ethnic groups/races.

At the top of New Spain society were the *peninsulars*. Peninsulars were Spanish-born individuals who immigrated to New Spain. They generally ran the regional and local government and owned the largest estates.

Just below the peninsulars were the *creoles*. The creoles were Mexican-born whites/Europeans, who usually came from wealthy families. Creoles often owned a lot of land and were well-represented in the trades, but rarely had government positions.

Mestizos were below the creoles and below the mestizos were the large number of Indians. Mexico also had a small but notable black African population, about 5 percent, which came to the land as slaves. Some of the Spanish men took African women as wives and/or mistresses, with the offspring of those unions being known as *mulattos*.

Although the colonial racial system was intended to keep the different ethnicities socially separated, it was not so rigid. There was no blood quantum or "one drop rule" as in North America, which gave much more "wiggle room" for mixed-race people to move to another classification.

Eventually, by the time Mexico attained its independence, most people began simply viewing themselves as "Mexicans."

Inspired by Washington and Jefferson

You can probably imagine that the legal and social system in Mexico led to tensions between the different ethnic groups, but most of that tension was directed at the peninsulars. The creoles wanted more power in the government. When the Jesuit order of the Catholic Church was expelled from New Spain in 1767, this angered the mestizos, who were heavily represented in the order. The Indians were also upset over their place in Mexican society, generally, and they were angry over the government's action against the Jesuits because they often served the poorest of society, which were often Indians.

Slavery was also still legal in Mexico, which was yet another social problem.

Inspired by the American and French Revolutions, the creoles began to question Spain's leadership, but they also feared being ruled by the mestizo and Indian majority. Unlike in America though, where revolution was led by the upper and middle classes, the Mexican Revolution was started by a priest who catered to the poor – Miguel Hidalgo y Costilla.

Hidalgo was deeply influenced by the American Revolution and the French Revolution of 1789, but he desired to make the Mexican Revolution unique to his country when he led to the poor to rise up in 1810.

It was too much for most of the creoles.

Hidalgo was captured and executed by the Spanish government in 1811, but the revolution he started had only just begun.

The Emperor of Mexico

So you know that Mexico was ruled by kings and queens for most of its early history. Aztec kings ruled most of Mexico before the Spanish arrived, and after they arrived, Spain's kings and queens were rulers of the land. But did you know that when Mexico finally achieved its independence from Spain in 1821, it was briefly ruled by a Mexican-born emperor?

This is just another interesting but little known fact of Mexico's history.

After Father Hidalgo's rebellion was suppressed, other small rebellions cropped up around Mexico. They eventually coalesced under the leadership of another mestizo priest named Jose Maria Morelos y Pavon. Most of Morelos' activities were focused west and south of Mexico City. Although he won several important battles, he too was captured and executed in 1815.

One of the military officers who pursued both priests and their ragtag armies was Agustin de Iturbide.

Iturbide was from a distinguished creole family, and like most creoles he harbored resentment toward the peninsulars for the preferential treatment they received from the crown. Iturbide and most of the other creoles, though, envisioned the future state of Mexico to be far less republican than the United States. Iturbide believed the Catholic Church should continue its influence and that the old social/racial order should remain essentially the same, but with the creoles joining the peninsulars at the top rung of the social ladder.

Iturbide got the support of the Church, military, and enough of the lower classes to become the leader of this new independence movement. The leaders developed what became known as the *Plan of Iguala*, which laid out the most important points of Mexico's new government: the social/racial class system was eliminated, slavery was abolished, the Roman Catholic Church was recognized as the state religion, and the government would be a constitutional monarchy, with an emperor as head of state.

Iturbide would become the Mexican Empire's first emperor on May 19, 1822.

When Iturbide became emperor, he wasted no time in becoming a dictator. He quickly dissolved congress, which angered many of his former allies, including General Antonio Santa Anna. You may have heard of him fighting a little place called the Alamo.

Iturbide was removed from power by his former allies on March 19, 1823, and he fled in exile to Italy. He made the mistake of returning to Mexico about a year later, thinking that any old wounds had healed.

He was wrong. On July 19, 1824, Agustin de Iturbide was executed by firing squad.

Don't Mess with Texas

The first few decades of the Mexican Republic were marked by turmoil and instability. Most of the old economic and ethnic problems still existed, and the central government in Mexico City was faced with the difficulty of being a country comprised of a patchwork of very different regions. Most of what is today the southwestern United States was part of Mexico, but it was underpopulated and often plagued by Comanche Indian raids. Mexico also had severe economic problems stemming from trade and lawlessness.

Mexico was a real mess in the early 1800s.

To add to all its problems, the government was extremely unstable, with the presidency changing hands thirty-six times from 1833 to 1855. General Santa Anna served eleven of those terms, virtually as a dictator shaping early modern Mexican history according to his will and personality.

In order to bring some stability to the country, Santa Anna decided to follow a Spanish policy of inviting Americans to settle lands north of the Rio Grande. It was believed that the industrious Americans could tame the territory without significantly changing the Mexican culture. So in 1821, a charter was given to American Moses Austin to bring three hundred American Catholic families to settle in what is now Texas.

There were of course provisions. The immigration would be controlled and limited, with all immigrants being Catholic and being required to learn Spanish. Slavery was discouraged and eventually outlawed to conform with Mexican law.

But none of this stopped slave-owning Protestant Americans from flooding into the fertile lands of Texas. By 1835 there were more than thirty thousand settlers in Texas, many of whom still felt a connection and loyalty to the United States, and none of whom had any feelings for Mexico.

Conflict was imminent.

On October 2, 1835, the Texans (as the American settlers in Texas referred to themselves) were in open rebellion. Santa Anna thought that he could lead a large force north of the Rio Grande, scaring most of the Texans into submission and massacring those who didn't surrender.

He was obviously wrong.

The Battle of the Alamo (from February 23 to March 6, 1836) saw General Santa Anna lead a force of nearly two thousand men massacre a small Texan force of only about two hundred fifty men. Although the Texans lost the battle, it also exposed Santa Anna's weaknesses and provided a rallying cry for future battles. On April 21, 1836, Texan General Sam Houston annihilated a Mexican force of about twelve hundred at San Jacinto, which effectively ended the war.

Texas became an independent nation, but there was still that matter of California.

The Bear Flag Revolt

Mexico may have been forced to give up Texas, but it surely wasn't going to give up the rest of its territory north of the Rio Grande. For a time, it looked like America would annex Texas and Mexico threatened war if this was done. But the debates over slavery slowed the issue north of the border.

For the leaders in Mexico though, Texas was still part of their republic. And to those Mexicans who did recognize Texas, the actual border wasn't even clear. The Texans claimed that the border was at the Rio Grande, while many Mexicans thought it was a few miles north at the Nueces River.

The strip of no-man's-land between the rivers became known as the Nueces Strip.

Seeing an opportunity to win more land for the United States, American President Zachary Taylor sent troops to Texas under the guise of protecting American citizens. As a small contingent of American soldiers patrolled the Nueces Strip on April 26, 1846, they were attacked by a large force of the Mexican Army, starting the Mexican-American War, which lasted until 1848.

The Americans invaded Mexico, took all of the territory that is now the American southwest, and established itself as the preeminent power in the Western Hemisphere. This loss marked the beginning of the end for Santa Anna's career as a leader, although he would briefly serve once more as Mexico's president from 1853 to 1855. Mexico had already lost Texas, and the territories it lost in 1848 were primarily desert and full of hostile Indians.

But there was that strip of land known as California.

Like Texas, California had been inundated with American immigrants from the 1820s, although Spanish settlers outnumbered them. In June of 1846, just after the Mexican-American War began, a group of Californian settlers led by William B. Ide rebelled against Mexican rule and flew a flag with a bear on it as their symbol. The revolt became known as the "Bear Flag Revolt" and the flag would later form the basis of the state of California's flag.

In 1948, Mexico lost ownership of California and Texas, along with the rest of the southwestern territories. About a month before the Mexican-American War ended, gold was discovered at Sutter's Mill, California, which sparked the California Gold Rush, bringing enormous wealth into the United States.

It was perhaps a cruel twist of fate that the gold was

discovered just as Mexico lost California. But as we'll see later, Mexico is full of plenty of "black gold."

The Reform War

By the mid-1800s it was obvious that Mexico had severe problems. Poverty continued to be an issue, but even worse were the social and political divisions within the country. On the one side you had the Liberal Party, which wanted to drastically reform Mexican society. The Liberals knew that the days of empire were long gone and that government policies should be focused on alleviating poverty through social programs and the occasional nationalization of foreign companies.

Their opposition, the Conservative Party, believed in courting foreign investment and keeping the status quo. The leaders of the party were beholden to "old money" business interests and the Catholic Church.

It was a clash that eventually became violent.

A new Mexican Constitution in 1857 guaranteed many Liberal reforms and also that a Liberal Party member, Benito Juarez, would become president in 1858.

The Liberals had already been in power for some time and, in addition to carrying out social programs such as confiscating Church land and nationalizing some foreign companies, the branches of government were firmly in the Liberal Party's hands.

This was too much for many in the Conservative Party.

Violence broke out in 1857 and quickly escalated into a full-fledged civil war which became known as the "Reform War." The Conservatives had the early advantage because most of Mexico's top military officers were in their camp.

But the Liberals were tenacious and had American support. Yeah, it always helps to have dollars pouring into your war effort.

The Liberals won the Reform War in 1860 and Juarez was re-elected president in 1861, but things were about to get real interesting. With the Civil War raging north of the border, the Conservatives decided to make their own play for foreign support.

About the Monroe Doctrine

Okay, we have to digress a little here and go back a few decades. We also have to cover a little American history before we can move on, but hopefully you'll remember most of this from your American history class.

Do you remember learning about the "Monroe Doctrine?"

This was a policy enacted by American President James Monroe in 1823 that stated the United States would use force if foreign powers attempted to colonize or recolonize the Western Hemisphere. Despite America's military weakness in the early 1800s, the policy was generally respected. The French briefly intervened in Mexico in the 1830s, but in December of 1861, as the United States was fighting itself, French forces arrived in Mexico.

The French emperor, Napoleon III, nephew of Napoleon Bonaparte, said that troops were there to make Mexico pay its outstanding debts. Many members of the Conservative Party were initially happy to see the French and even worked with them. But any good will the French may have received quickly evaporated when they began killing innocent Mexicans.

Just as Cortés had done more than three hundred years earlier, the French landed in Veracruz and marched to Mexico City.

And there was nothing the Monroe Doctrine could do to stop them!

The Origins of Cinco de Mayo

Do you really known what Cinco de Mayo is all about? Sure, you probably know it is celebrated every May 5 and that there are specials on Corona and Dos Equis at your favorite bar that day But did you know that it has to do with the French Invasion of Mexico in 1861?

After initial negotiations broke down between the Mexican and French governments over the money Mexico owed, French troops began their march to Mexico City. Mexican General Ignacio Zaragosa brought a sizable Mexican force to meet the French advance, but they were soundly defeated and retreated to the town of Puebla City. When the French troops arrived on May 5, 1862, the Mexicans were waiting, with plenty of defensive fortifications and the locals firmly on their side.

The battle was a resounding victory for the Mexicans and became a rallying cry for the country. In the one hundred fifty-plus years since, the commemoration of the victory has become a national holiday in Mexico and an important celebration for Mexican-Americans and Mexicans living in the United States. It has also obviously become a good way for bars, liquor stores, and supermarkets to sell beer—nearly as much beer is sold in the United States for Cinco de Mayo as it is for the Super Bowl.

But how important was the Mexican victory at Puebla City?

Cinco de Mayo is often mistakenly confused with Mexican Independence Day, which happened on September 16, 1810. Independence Day was politically and historically more important as it marked the beginning of the modern state of Mexico.

So if Cinco de Mayo isn't about Mexican independence, then does it mark the expulsion of the French from Mexico? No, it doesn't. The French remained in Mexico until 1867, but the Mexican victory at Puebla City did slow the French advance for a year.

And most importantly, it provided a psychological victory for the Mexican people. Mexicans saw that when the various classes of their often divided country worked together, they could overcome some pretty major odds.

So the next time you're enjoying a few brews with your friends on May 5, you can tell them the real story behind the celebration.

Another Caudillo

In order to understand the political history of most Latin American countries, especially Mexico, it is important to understand the idea of the *caudillo*. In Latin American culture, a caudillo is a powerful man whose power is the result of his personality and charisma, which is often referred to as *caudillismo*. Iturbide was one of Mexico's first caudillos and Santa Anna is perhaps the best known.

But the country's greatest caudillo came to power after the French were expelled from Mexico—Porfirio Diaz.

Diaz was born in rural Mexico in 1830 to a white father and a mestizo mother, which made him a *castizo*. He found his place in the military and served against the French in the 1860s, advancing to the rank of general and making many important connections along the way.

After attempting an unsuccessful rebellion in 1872, Diaz was given amnesty and served in Congress before traveling to the United States where he plotted another rebellion.

His second attempt at overthrowing the presidency failed, so he went back to the United States to organize again.

The third time was a charm.

Diaz became President of Mexico after overthrowing Sebastian Lerdo in 1876. Diaz served as president until one of his allies was elected in 1880. Then, in 1884, Diaz was elected once more and he served as president until 1911.

Needless to say, Diaz's hold on power was not exactly legal.

There was definitely plenty of opposition to Diaz, but he was a smart guy who knew how to work the system. He kept Mexico's many political and social factions feuding with each other, and early in his rule the Mexican economy drastically improved, largely due to foreign investment.

As long as the economy was good, the middle class in Mexico City didn't say much.

But by the early 1900s, the economy wasn't doing as well and Diaz's corruption couldn't be contained much longer. In 1910, the year of Mexico's centennial, Diaz "allowed" Francisco Madero to run against him in the presidential election.

The fraud in this election was so overwhelming that news of it couldn't be contained. The often warring factions of Mexican society suddenly had a common enemy—Diaz. Knowing that his time was up, Diaz resigned from office on May 25, 1911. He fled the country soon thereafter.

Mexico was suddenly thrust into another revolution!

Pancho Villa and the Mexican Revolution

The Mexican Revolution may have started with the best intentions, but it quickly turned into an orgy of violence. Francisco Madero overthrew Diaz, but he didn't have much time to enjoy his time at the top as he was murdered in 1913. The reins of power were then assumed by General Victoriano Huerta, who was reluctantly supported by American business interests.

You see, between 1904 and 1913, Mexican oil production rose from over two hundred twenty thousand barrels to nearly twenty-six million. Mexico was also a leading rubber and sugar producer, and its railway system was either built or partially owned by American firms.

Huerta promised his supporters he would bring back order—and profits.

But once Pandora's box of revolution was opened, there was no going back!

You've probably heard the name Pancho Villa at least once in your life. Maybe it was at a popular Mexican restaurant that used his name, and an image of him wearing a sombrero, to sell Mexican-American food. Well, he was a real person and he was a real thorn in the side of Huerta and American business interests.

Villa led a revolt of the poor, mainly *peons*, in the northern state of Chihuahua. As Villa's force began to revolt, Emiliano Zapata led a similar revolt of Indians and *peons* in the southern Mexican states. So you're probably wondering, what is a peon?

You've no doubt heard (or even used) the word peon to describe a lowly worker at a business. Well, a peon was a person forced to work for a wealthy landowner in Spanish America. It was a step above slavery; the workers didn't actually have freedom since they had no real options. No real options until Villa and Zapata came to town!

As the revolution caught steam, Villa's army became known as the "Constitutionalist Army." It created enough problems for American business interests to lead to a U.S. Marine landing at Veracruz on April 21, 1914. The Marine landing actually helped Villa, as it led to Heurta being removed from power and the Constitutionalists taking Mexico City.

But since the Mexican Revolution was more like a civil war in many ways, the various factions that were united against the government began fighting among themselves. In an effort to survive—and possibly to unite—the factions under his leadership, Villa did a series of border raids, some of which killed citizens in New Mexico on March 9, 1916.

The raids were too much for American President Woodrow Wilson. Villa had to go.

The U.S. Army launched a punitive expedition into Chihuahua in the spring and summer of 1916, ostensibly to capture and punish Villa, but it also provided the Americans with a "warm-up" for their involvement in World War I.

Relative order was restored in Mexico and a new constitution was ratified in February of 1917. But Villa and Zapata kept fighting: Villa was assassinated in 1923, leaving behind at least twenty-three wives and an untold number of children, while Zapata was assassinated in 1919.

Guys like Villa and Zapata were relics of the past that the new leader of Mexico had no problem eliminating.

By Hook or By Crook

As our survey of Mexico's long and fascinating history is coming close to an end, I'm sure a few things stand out to you. First, Mexico is a pretty diverse place. A lot of different people have contributed to Mexico's history, which has made it pretty interesting and at times troublesome. From the various Mesoamerican peoples to the numerous social classes and ethnic groups of modern times, Mexico has been home to a variety of different groups.

Second, Mexico has experienced volatile and at times turbulent political history. Widespread human sacrifice, invasions, rebellions, and assassinations have marked Mexican history from ancient times to now. And many of these problems continue into the present.

In the years immediately following the Mexican Revolution, many of the influential survivors began brainstorming a way in which they could hold power and follow through with some of the revolution's objectives. Their answer was to form a political party. The Partido Nacional Revolucionario (National Revolutionary Party, or PNR) formed in 1929 as the apparent answer to the problems the Mexican Revolution veterans and Mexico faced. In 1946, the PNR changed its name to the Partido Revolucionario Institucional (Institutional Revolutionary Party, or PRI), which is what it is known as today.

In order to understand post-Revolution Mexico you have to understand the PRI.

After forming, the PNR/PRI quickly came to power through a variety of methods. It opened offices on the local and state as well as the federal level, made alliances in the labor unions, and formed coalitions with smaller political parties. It carefully crafted its image to appeal to the middle and working classes by using the colors of the Mexican flag in its logo. Once in federal power, it enacted policies that were popular with all classes and ethnic groups in Mexico, such as nationalizing the oil companies. The move to nationalize the oil companies before World War II proved to be extremely popular as most saw it as "sticking it to the Yankees!"

The PRI held nearly absolute power in Mexico from 1929 to 2000, but not necessarily because it was the most popular party. In places where the PRI was less popular, voter fraud was rampant, intimidation at the polls was common, and opposition candidates were routinely declared ineligible or even arrested.

The PRI knew how to stuff ballot boxes, and when that didn't work they would even declare elections null and void.

Eventually the PRI was toppled from power in legitimate elections, but it continues to be a major force in Mexican politics.

A Smuggler's Paradise

Mexico has been a smuggler's paradise for almost one hundred years. The cheap prices in Mexico and the demand and higher prices in the United States has led to an untold number of smugglers trying to bring booze, drugs, and people illegally across the international border. Until the 2000s, though, the situation was somewhat under control by the Mexican and American governments.

However, that was all about to change, starting in the 1990s.

Cocaine, marijuana, and heroin are just three illicit drugs that are cheap and plentiful south of the border but are expensive and in demand in the United States. Powerful Columbian cartels grew and manufactured these drugs for years, either flying them into the United States or smuggling them on land via Mexico.

But the United States' war on drugs changed all of that by the late 1990s. Most of the Columbian kingpins were toppled and the smuggling routes through Miami were closed. But there were still plenty of drugs to be moved, so smaller organizations on the U.S.-Mexican border, such as the Sinaloa and Gulf cartels, stepped up to fill the shoes of the Columbians.

The Mexican cartels proved to be more efficient and industrious when it came to smuggling and even more ruthless when dealing with enemies, which by 2006 included the Mexican government.

The result has been a full-scale civil war in parts of Mexico: More than four thousand Mexican police and soldiers have been killed in the violence and nearly thirteen thousand cartel members have died. Tragically, one hundred thousand-plus civilians have also lost their lives in the violence that has made some parts of Mexico unlivable. Unfortunately, due to a number of reasons, the cartel violence in Mexico shows no signs of stopping anytime soon.

RANDOM FACTS

1. The period of Porfirio Diaz's rule over Mexico is often known as the "Porfiriato." The term was first coined by Mexican historian Daniel Villegas in the 1950s.

2. Although Pancho Villa is known to have had twenty-three wives, he may have had as many as seventy-five. Villa clearly didn't believe in divorce.

3. Coronado's wife Beatriz was only fifteen when he married her. She was from a wealthy family, which helped fund Coronado's expeditions. The couple had four sons and five daughters.

4. During his exile from Mexico, General Santa Anna lived in Cuba and the United States. He is credited with introducing chewing gum to the United States in the 1860s. It was produced from chicle, which the Mayans used for gum. Yes, that is where Chiclets gets its name!

5. Vicente Fox was the first post-Revolution president not to be a member of the PRI when he was elected in 2000. He was a member of the National Action Party.

6. The first line in the United States Marines' "Marines' Hymn," "From the Halls of

Montezuma," is a reference to the Battle of Chapultepec on September 12-13, 1847, during the Mexican-American War. The Marines took Chapultepec Castle, which the Spanish built over an Aztec temple. The victory gave the Americans a clear shot at Mexico City.

7. Cinco de Mayo is believed to have been first celebrated by Mexican miners in California in 1863. Although celebrated in Mexico, Cinco de Mayo is much more popular in the United States.

8. The Treaty of Guadeloupe Hidalgo officially ended the Mexican-American War. The treaty was signed by representatives of both nations in the town of Villa de Guadeloupe Hidalgo, which is now a neighborhood of Mexico City.

9. Most of the Mexican drug cartels are named after the region where they are from or the person who started it, but one has a particularly strange name—Knights Templar cartel. The Knights Templar cartel takes its name from a medieval European Crusader order, which they claim to admire. The Knights Templar cartel claims to follow a code and to be Christians!

10. Although Mexico is not generally thought to have much of an African influence, Afro-Mexicans today comprise over 1 percent of the overall population and more than 3 percent of the population of the state of Veracruz. An

ethnically mixed society, DNA tests show that the majority of modern Mexicans have up to 5 percent African DNA.

11. After the Reform War ended in January of 1861, France, Spain, and the United Kingdom signed the Convention of London on October 31 of that year. The Convention called for a potential invasion of Mexico to collect loans owed to the three countries. France used the treaty as a means to expand its empire.

12. The Zapatista Army of National Liberation is a communist guerilla group that formed in 1994 in the Mexican state of Chiapas. The group takes its name and some of its ideology from Emiliano Zapata of the Mexican Revolution.

13. *Viva Zapata!* is a 1952 biopic film of Emiliano Zapata. The screenplay was written by legendary American author John Steinbeck and Zapata was played by Marlon Brando.

14. Tejano is the term for Hispanics who supported and/or stayed in Texas after it gained its independence from Mexico.

15. The Mexican Empire technically had two emperors: Agustin de Iturbide (Agustin I) and Maximilian I. They were not of the same dynasty, however, and their rule was separated by about forty years.

16. A man named Count Maximilian Gustav Albrecht Richard Augustin von Götzen-Iturbide claims he is a direct maternal descendent of Agustin Iturbide. He also claims to be the representative of the Imperial House of Mexico, though he is not actively pursuing any power in Mexico.

17. Like Mexico City, most of the first cities the Spanish built were constructed near, or on top of, Mesoamerican cities.

18. The royal European dynasties that ruled Mexico when it was part of New Spain were the Hapsburgs and Bourbons.

19. On July 1, 2012, the PRI returned to power when Enrique Nieto won the presidency. The honeymoon didn't last long, though, as the PRI was soundly defeated in the 2018 general elections.

20. After Victoriano Huerta was exiled, he became involved in a plot with Germany to regain power in Mexico and then join Germany's side in World War I. He was imprisoned by while attempting to enter Mexico from New Mexico and died in an American prison in 1916.

Test Yourself – Questions

1. The "Bear Flag Revolt" took place in which American state that was once part of Mexico?

    a. Florida
    b. Texas
    c. California

2. This is the acronym of Mexico's leading political party from 1929 to 2000:

    a. DRI
    b. PRI
    c. SAS

3. Along with Poncho Villa, this man was the other major leader of the Mexican Revolution:

    a. Emiliano Zapata
    b. Santa Anna
    c. Agustin de Iturbide

4. Cinco de Mayo is a celebration of what?

    a. Mexican Independence
    b. Mexico's Aztec heritage
    c. A Mexican battle victory over the French

5. The civil war in Mexico that took place from 1857 to 1860 between the Liberal Party and the Conservative Party is known as the:

    a. Political War
    b. Reform War
    c. Northern Mexican War

Answers

1. c
2. b
3. a
4. c
5. b

CHAPTER THREE

MEXICO'S GEOGRAPHY, TOPOGRAPHY, AND CLIMATE

When most people think about the geography of Mexico they tend to focus on the physical geography: the mountains, deserts, oceans, and hot climate. Yes, Mexico has all of those geographic features, but it also has so much more. There are jungles in the southern states, and the country has many different climate zones. Also, there is a lot more to geography than just physical features and climate. Geography includes how ethnic and political groups are distributed. As you already know from the first two chapters, Mexico has its fair share of ethnic and political diversity. Mexico is also home to quite a few natural resources. Did you know that Mexico is a major oil-producing country? So follow along as we take a trip through Mexico, from north to south and from east to west.

71

Isthmuses and Peninsulas

Among Mexico's most notable geographic features, at least when you look at the country on a map, is the fact that it's comprised of isthmuses and peninsulas. An isthmus is simply a narrow piece of land that connects two larger pieces of land. Obviously Mexico isn't narrow (it is the world's thirteenth largest country), but it is narrower than the United States to its north. And when compared to its Central American neighbors to its south, Mexico is narrower than Colombia. So technically, it is part of a larger isthmus.

But Mexico also has its own notable isthmus.

The Isthmus of Tehuantepec is in the far southern part of Mexico, primarily in the states of Veracruz and Oaxaca. It is in a generally east-west orientation and is between longitude 94° and 96° west. The Isthmus of Tehuantepec is only about one hundred twenty-four miles at its widest part, which makes it the narrowest section of Mexico.

The other features you probably notice when you look at a map of Mexico are the peninsulas. A peninsula is land mass that is surrounded on three sides by water. In the United States, Florida is a peninsula and so is Michigan, which is actually two peninsulas.

Mexico has two notable peninsulas: Baja California and the Yucatan Peninsula. Baja California is the part of Mexico that extends south from California, while the Yucatan Peninsula is the large peninsula located in southeast Mexico. The Yucatan is where many of the Mayan cities were and is also where Cancun is located.

The United Mexican States

You probably didn't know that the official name of the country of Mexico is Estados Unidos Mexicanos, or United Mexican States. Similarly to how most people refer to the United States as simply "America," the majority of people refer to the United Mexican States as "Mexico."

And the administrative geographic similarities with the United States don't end there.

Like the United States, Mexico is comprised of separate states—thirty-one to be exact. Also like in the U.S., each of the individual Mexican states has a degree of political autonomy. Each state has its own constitution and congress. Consequently, these individual states are allowed to pass laws that are not covered by the federal government and that do not conflict with the Constitution of 1917.

Besides the thirty-one individual states, Mexico City is an autonomous zone. It used to be the federal district, but in 2016 the Federal District was eliminated and Mexico City was given the same status as a state.

Mexico City is where the presidential palace, Congress, and the Supreme Court are located.

Each state elects representatives to sit in the national Congress, which has two chambers like the United States. One notable difference between the U.S.'s and Mexico's political geography, though, is that Mexico doesn't elect its president through an electoral college system.

Mexico's National Flag

Mexico has used different versions of the current national flag, "Bandera de Mexico," since its independence from Spain in 1821. The first version of the flag was authorized by Iturbide to have a tricolored red, white, and green design with an eagle wearing a crown in the middle of the white stripe. In 1823, the crown was removed and a serpent was placed in the eagle's talons. The cactus that the eagle is perched on was added by the French and was—perhaps somewhat surprisingly—kept after they were expelled.

Other minor changes were made until 1968, when it became the flag that it is today.

So what do the colors and the figures on the flag symbolize?

Well, hopefully you remember from the last two chapters that the eagle and the snake come from the

Aztec legend of the founding of Tenochtitlan. The combined images comprise Mexico's coat of arms, symbolizing the country's pre-Columbian history as well as its Spanish heritage—the Spanish viewed the legend and the later coat of arms as a metaphor for good defeating evil.

The symbolism of the colors, like that of most national flags, is less concrete and has evolved over the last two hundred years. The most common interpretation is that the green color originally represented Mexico's struggle for independence from Spain and its pre-Colombian heritage, while the red was symbolic of its still-strong ties to Europe. The white was representative of the Catholic Church and its spiritual purity.

No matter how the meaning of the flag's colors is interpreted, there is no denying that Mexico has one of the world's most unique and instantly recognizable flags.

Did You Know Mexico Is a Major Oil Producer?

When most people think of major oil-producing nations they think of the Arabian countries, Russia, or even Venezuela, but certainly not Mexico. Right? Actually, Mexico is a major oil-producing country, with the seventeenth largest oil reserves beneath its soil and off its shores. It is the eleventh largest producer of oil in the world and the fourth largest in the Americas. Oil exports are also 10 percent of Mexico's total earnings in exports, so oil is clearly a major part of Mexico's economy.

Does that mean Mexico has its own J.R. Ewing type of oil barons?

No, not really.

You see, all oil in Mexico is owned and extracted by the state-owned Pemex (Mexican Petroleum). Mexico's 1917 Constitution gave total mineral rights to the Mexican government. But the country was reliant on foreigners, primarily Americans, with more expertise in the industry to extract the resources. In 1938, partly in an effort to curry favor with some of its constituents, President Lazaro Cardenas del Rio and the PRI (remember those guys?) decided to nationalize all foreign oil companies. The government then started its own company—Pemex—which has had complete control over the Mexican oil industry ever since.

Most of the Mexican oil fields are in three geographic clusters. The northern parts of the states of Tamaulipas and Nuevo Leon, near the international border with Texas, are a major area. There are also many land operations near the coast in the states of Tamaulipas and Veracruz and several offshore platforms in the Gulf of Mexico off the coasts of the states of Tabasco and Campeche.

Surrounded by Mountains

One of Mexico's most defining and noticeable geographic features is its two major mountain ranges that follow close to the coastlines, essentially enclosing most of the country within them. These ranges are the Sierra Madre Occidental and the Sierra Madre Oriental. Their names translate to "Mother of Mountains," with Occidental meaning "western" and Oriental meaning "eastern."

The Sierra Madre Occidental is actually part of what is known as the North American Cordillera, or continuous mountain chain, that runs from Alaska through Mexico. So that means the Sierra Madre Occidental is actually part of the Rocky Mountains. The northern end of the Sierra Madre Occidental is in the state of Sonora near the Arizona border, and it runs for about nine hundred miles south before terminating in the smaller Sierra Madre del Sur range in southern Mexico. Elevations in the range are more than eight thousand feet, with the highest peak being Cerro Mohinora (at 10,827 feet) in the state of Chihuahua.

The Sierra Madre Oriental (the Sierra Madre Occidental's brother, or sister range) is a little shorter in length, at about six hundred miles, but its peaks are higher. The highest summit in the Sierra Madre Oriental is Cerro San Rafael (at 12,139 feet) in the state of Coahuila. The Sierra Madre Oriental's northern end is the Rio Grande in the state of Coahuila near the Texas border.

The ranges are also quite wide in some areas—the Occidental is one hundred fifty miles in some sections and the Oriental is three hundred miles wide in the northern part. The heights of the peaks of both ranges, and the fact that they are so wide, means that if you are in just about any part of the Mexican Plateau between these two ranges, you will be able to see mountains.

You should be able to get a great view from just about anywhere in Mexico.

Mexico and the Tropic of Cancer

By now you should know that when it comes to Mexico, there is far more than meets the eyes. Its history is long and varied, its people and topography are diverse, and its climate can also vary dramatically depending on where you are in the country.

A lot of that has to do with the Tropic of Cancer.

For those of you who aren't geography nerds, the Tropic of Cancer is the most northern circle of latitude where the sun can be directly overhead during the summer solstice. It actually moves slightly, but is currently at the twenty-fourth parallel and cuts almost directly through the middle of Mexico, effectively dividing the country into a temperate zone to the north and a tropic zone to the south.

The temperatures in both zones actually vary very little throughout the year. For example, on the Yucatan Peninsula temperatures range anywhere from 70°F to 80°F and above, with only about a ten-degree variation throughout the year.

The same is true in Mexico City, which only averages a low of 42°F in January and a high of 78°F in May. The climate of Mexico City is further affected by its high elevation—it is located at seven thousand five hundred feet above sea level.

The Sierra Madre mountain chains also influence Mexico's overall climate. The mountains are high enough that some retain snow year-round, which can also affect the precipitation, with the Mexican Plateau between the two chains receiving significantly less rainfall than the coastal regions and southernmost states, which are in a tropical rainforest zone.

So if you're planning on taking a trip to Mexico, be sure to take a coat if you're going to the mountains or Mexico City. But you can pretty much just pack shorts if you're going to the coasts or the far southern states.

Wolves, Jaguars, and Tomatoes

Wolves, jaguars, and cacti are just some of the fauna and flora you'll find in Mexico. The country is home to more than two hundred thousand species of animals of all sizes and types. And more than sixty-five thousand square miles of Mexico is protected land, which includes national parks, biosphere reserves, and wildlife sanctuaries.

Among the larger mammals native to Mexico is the Mexican wolf. The Mexican wolf is a subspecies of the gray wolf and although it was once very common, it is now endangered. Less than fifty live in the wild in the states of Sonora and Chihuahua.

Perhaps the most interesting and historically important of all animals native to Mexico is the jaguar. The jaguar is the biggest cat in the Americas and can be found in the wild from Argentina to northern Mexico. In pre-Columbian times, the jaguar was an important spiritual animal for the different Mesoamerican peoples, especially the Aztecs whose warriors emulated the strength and agility of the animal. In present day Mexico, jaguars are found in sizable numbers in the rainforests of the south, but can also be found in coastal areas and even in the mountains and deserts of the north.

The cactus that is featured on the Mexican flag can be found throughout most of the northern desert and plateau states, but once you get south of Mexico City the flora changes quite a bit. Palm trees and taller grasses are the norm in the south, but all throughout the country you can find a number of fruits and vegetables growing there as they have for centuries.

Besides corn/maize, tomatoes, avocados, numerous beans and chilies, chocolate, and vanilla are all native to Mexico. It's hard to imagine what cooking would be like without some of these plants.

Can you imagine Italian food without tomatoes? As much as tomato sauce and tomatoes are associated with Italian food, they didn't become a part of the Italian diet until the late 1500s.

Finally, how can we talk about Mexico's flora and fauna without mentioning the monarch butterfly? Every year, monarchs make summer in Canada and the United States a little brighter. Toward the end of the summer, monarchs begin their long migration south which, for many, ends at the Monarch Butterfly Biosphere Reserve in the Mexican state of Michoacán, about sixty miles north of Mexico City. There are eight total colonies of wintering monarchs in Mexico, but only two are open to the public.

Those who have visited the monarch colonies say it is definitely worth the travel and is a truly wonderful experience.

Mexico's Ground is Alive with Activity

One of Mexico's most destructive geographic features is the very active seismic zone that exists under much of it. Like the United States, Mexico is on the North American Plate. However, just off its Pacific coast is the Cocos Plate. I won't get too technical on you about tectonic plates, but it is important to know that all of them move. In Mexico's case, the North American Plate and the Cocos Plate are colliding in their movement; this has created hundreds of recent earthquakes as well as numerous volcanoes.

We'll get to the volcanoes in a little bit.

Many of Mexico's earthquakes happen in the Pacific Ocean but are powerful enough to be felt—and cause damage—hundreds of miles inland. The most destructive earthquake in modern times took place on September 9, 1985, off the coast of Michoacán; it was strong enough to cause immense damage in Mexico City. The massive quake created a huge tsunami that killed thousands and created millions of dollars of damage to the capital city.

Many of the deaths resulted from old buildings that weren't up to proper earthquake code. In the years since the 1985 quake, the Mexican government has dedicated a lot of time and resources to keeping buildings up to proper code and making sure the public knows what to do in case of an earthquake.

The government's planning seems to have worked. In 2017, exactly thirty-two years after the massive 1985 catastrophe, Mexico City was hit with another large earthquake. This time, only three hundred seventy people are recorded as having died.

Please Don't Blow Your Top!

Just to the south of Mexico City is a mountain chain known as Sierra Nevada (Snowy Mountains) to the locals, but to geographers and geologists it is the Trans-Mexican Volcanic Belt. As the name indicates, the mountain range is actually a chain of volcanic mountains. The local name also indicates that many of these mountains are snowcapped year-round, which provides a beautiful backdrop to Mexico City—if the smog levels are low enough, that is!

The chain traverses Mexico from coast-to-coast for over six hundred miles, with its western terminus being the southernmost point of the Sierra Madre Occidental. The belt has just about every type of volcano, including monogenetic volcanoes, shield volcanoes, lava domes, and calderas. Many of these volcanoes are active, and have been for centuries, with several given names by the Aztecs.

Colima Volcano, which is located on the eastern part of the belt in the state of Jalisco, last erupted in 2017. Experts believe it erupted several times in the pre-Columbian era. And it has erupted forty times since

1576. An eruption in 1585 actually blocked out the sun and subsequent eruptions resulted in deaths. Fortunately, the more recent eruptions didn't cause any fatalities.

The bigger volcanoes often combine with the man-made air pollution to reduce visibility and cause major problems for people with respiratory problems. When the levels get toxically high, the young, old, and those suffering from respiratory ailments are advised to stay inside or wear a mask when they leave the house.

A Variety of Languages

Since you now know about Mexico's long and interesting history, you can probably figure out that Spanish is the country's national language. It is the language used by the government and the primary language used in the daily lives of the vast majority of Mexicans. With over one hundred twenty-six million people, Mexico is by far the most populous Spanish-speaking nation in the world. Spain, the mother country of all Spanish speakers, has only forty-seven million inhabitants and Argentina, the largest Spanish-speaking country in South America, has forty-five million people.

So you're probably wondering, if the *vast majority* of Mexicans speak Spanish as their primary language, what other languages are spoken in Mexico?

If you were to visit Mexico City, you'd no doubt hear dozens of different languages, sometimes in a single day. The capital and financial center is home to expatriates from around the world. But Mexico's true linguistic diversity is in the more remote areas and the rainforests of the south.

The Mexican government recognizes sixty-eight national languages, of which sixty-three are indigenous or Indian. Those languages are also subdivided into several hundred dialects. The Aztec language, Nahuatl, is still spoken by about 1 percent of the population, with the heaviest concentration of speakers in and around Mexico City, which was of course the heart of the Aztec Empire.

Around one million people also speak variations of the Mayan language, with the heaviest concentration of speakers living on the Yucatan Peninsula. Many of these indigenous people are bilingual, though the pressures of modern society have led to a steady decrease in the use and knowledge of all indigenous languages in Mexico.

The states with the most, and highest concentration of, indigenous-language speakers are in central and southern Mexico. The state of Oaxaca has the highest percentage of indigenous speakers at 1,165,186 people, or 34 percent of its population. The state of Yucatan is close behind at 30 percent, but it is much smaller in comparison, with just over five hundred thousand indigenous speakers.

The northern states, especially those bordering the United States, have the lowest percentages and numbers of indigenous speakers. The state of Sonora, which borders Arizona, has the highest percentage in the region with 2.5 percent of its population speaking an indigenous language.

Hurricanes Are Named After a Mayan Storm God

Hurricanes affect millions of Americans every year on the Atlantic and Gulf coasts. But did you know that just as many Mexicans—often more—are adversely affected by hurricanes every year? You see, unlike the United States, which gets hit only by Atlantic hurricanes, Mexico gets hit by both Atlantic and Pacific hurricanes from June to November. In fact, nearly every state is susceptible to heavy rains and/or damage from hurricanes.

And Mexico has had some calamitous hurricanes in modern times.

Hurricane Janet killed over eight hundred people and caused over $45 million in damages when it made landfall in the Yucatan in 1955. More recently, Hurricane Gilbert left two hundred people dead in 1988, and Hurricane Wilma cost the country $10 billion when it made landfall on the Yucatan Peninsula in 2005.

Clearly, hurricanes are a big part of Mexico's geography and culture, which can be traced by to its country pre-Columbian past.

According to the Mayan creation myth, *Popol Vuh*, the god Hurucan is described as the "heart of heaven" and is personified as a storm. Experts believe that the name of the god was then used by the Spanish, who had little familiarity with hurricanes in Europe, to refer to the massive storms.

So just remember, if you're planning a trip to Mexico between June and November—especially to the Yucatan—make sure to regularly check the weather reports!

What's That Peninsula That's Connected to California?

You've probably looked at a map before and noticed that a long peninsula juts into the Pacific Ocean south of the U.S.-Mexican border at San Ysidro. You may also know that it is called Baja California and that it is a Mexican state.

But it is actually two Mexican states—Baja California and Baja California Sur, which is the southern of the two (sur means "south" in Spanish). Together, these two states comprise the Baja California Peninsula.

The peninsula is separate from the rest of Mexico by the Gulf of California to its west and the Colorado River, which empties into the Gulf of California. A thin strip of desert land connects the peninsula to the state of Sonora, but it is actually joined to California by better roads.

The peninsula is fairly long, at about seven hundred sixty miles. However, it is quite narrow, ranging from one hundred twenty-five miles at its widest to a meager twenty-five miles at its narrowest. Because of the shape of the peninsula, most of the major roads are north-south. The peninsula is also home to several small mountain ranges, which are collectively known as the Peninsular Ranges. The peninsula's mountains provide scenic backdrops to its many beautiful beaches and are a common destination for hikers.

In fact, Baja California and Baja California Sur are a prime destination for many people. The two states generally have less unemployment, far less crime, and generally boast a higher standard of living than most of the other Mexican states, making them an attractive location many Mexicans and Central American immigrants. Americans are also drawn to the Baja for the cheaper living, nice beaches, and the close proximity to San Diego—Tijuana is often considered part of the San Diego metropolitan area.

We'll talk more about some of the prime vacation spots in the Baja Peninsula in a later chapter.

Water Is a True Commodity in Mexico

When you look at a map of Mexico, you probably notice all of the water around it. The Caribbean Sea is on its east coast and the Pacific Ocean is on its west coast. But those are saltwater oceans and not much good for drinking water. So what is Mexico's freshwater situation?

Well, Mexico has about one hundred fifty rivers, most of which empty into the Pacific Ocean, but most of their volume comes from just five rivers—the Usumacinta, Grijalva, Papaloapan, Coatzacoalcos, and Panuco rivers. The first four of these rivers empty into the Caribbean in southeast Mexico. Most of Mexico's population, though, lives in central and northern Mexico, which is arid and has few sources of fresh water.

So how does most of Mexico get its drinking water?

The source and quality of drinking water can range widely between the municipalities in Mexico. Most cities get their public water through a mains feed system, while smaller towns source from local water springs and wells. Ranches, farms, and more remote locations use wells and many places still use cisterns.

Many of the larger resorts use a combination and also have plenty of bottled water on hand for their guests.

If you're visiting Mexico, you should find out about the source of the water you're drinking and if it's potable. Even if the locals say it is, their bodies may be more used to a lower quality than you are, so you may want to go with bottled water in order to avoid Montezuma's revenge.

The Laguna Salada Is the Lowest Point in Mexico

If you travel about nineteen miles west of Mexicali, the capital of Baja California, into the Sonora Desert, you might come across the Laguna Salada.

Or you might miss it!

The Laguna Salada, or "Salty Lagoon," is a mostly dry, salty lake that is located a few miles south of the main highway. It is also the lowest geographic point in Mexico at about thirty-three feet below sea level. Although the region is extremely dry, when it does rain the lagoon can fill up to become a lake that is thirty-seven miles long and eleven miles wide. (It rarely fills up this completely though.) The lagoon is flanked on either side by mountains and has, in recent years, become a popular destination spot for travelers looking for scenic and not-so-commercialized destinations.

Although there are plenty of motels and other facilities in nearby Mexicali, visitors to the Laguna Salada find that it is best for them to pack their own lunches. There are several trails, some local outfitters, and even relaxing hot springs for hikers to enjoy after checking out the lagoon.

But for the most part, the Laguna Salada looks much like it did when Coronado traveled through the area nearly five hundred years ago.

RANDOM FACTS

1. The highest point in Mexico is Pico de Orizaba, which is 18,491 feet. Pico do Orizaba is a dormant volcano that straddles the states of Veracruz and Puebla. Despite it being located in southern Mexico's subtropical zone, Pico de Orizaba's summit is snow-covered year-round due to its elevation.

2. Although oil exports are a vital part of Mexico's economy, it is only fourth in the country's top exports. Automobiles and parts are actually Mexico's number one export.

3. Mexico is the world's leading supplier of avocados. It exports more than two million tons of the delicious fruit every year.

4. Mexico City is not only the capital city of Mexico, but also the country's largest city. It has nearly nine million inhabitants with more than twenty million living in its metropolitan area, making it the largest metro area in the Americas.

5. The Rio Grande, which separates much of Mexico from the United States, is the country's longest river.

6. Mexico only borders three countries: the United States, Belize, and Guatemala.

7. Although much of early Mexican history was focused Lake Texcoco, Mexico doesn't have many natural lakes. After the Spanish built Mexico City on Lake Texcoco, Lake Chapala became Mexico's largest natural lake. It is located in the state of Michoacán and covers more than four hundred twenty square miles.

8. Mexico has one of the best developed highway systems in Latin America. Besides local and state highways, Mexico has a federal highway system of controlled access, free and toll, highways that is similar to the United States interstate system.

9. Mexico has dozens of seaports on both the Pacific and Caribbean coasts that accommodate freight and passenger ships. The busiest freight port is located in Lazaro Cardenas, Michoacán.

10. Like the continental United States, Mexico has four time zones: Southeast (corresponds to US. Eastern), Central, Pacific (corresponds to U.S. Mountain), and Northwest (corresponds to U.S. Pacific).

11. Chiapas is the southernmost state of Mexico and has also been the location of guerrilla and paramilitary violence over the last twenty-five years.

12. Oil and other valuable mineral resources in Mexico has been a double-edged sword. The

commodities have brought the country plenty of money, but they have also led to severe deforestation in many of the southern states. For instance, Tabasco was reduced from nearly half tree cover in 1940 to less than 10 percent by the 1980s.

13. Although the people of Mesoamerica developed sophisticated calendars, studied the stars, and devised writing, they never developed cartography (mapmaking).

14. The Sierra Mixteca is the name of the region in south-central Mexico where the Sierra Madre Oriental, the Sierra Nevada, and the Sierra Madre Del Sur mountains converge.

15. You may find it hard to believe that the three most agriculturally productive Mexican states are the most arid: Baja California, Sonora, and Sinaloa. Although these are desert states, with the help of irrigation, their long, dry growing seasons produce an array of crops.

16. As with most countries that have a federal government, each of the Mexican states has its own seal and flag.

17. Mexico shares a border with the United States that is more than two thousand miles long, but its border with Belize and Guatemala is only about seven hundred miles combined.

18. An archipelago in the Pacific Ocean called the Revillagigedo Islands is owed by Mexico. Less than one hundred people live on the islands.

19. Besides oil, Mexico is a major producer of several other minerals, including: zinc, silver, copper, gold, and lead.

20. Several species of spider monkeys, which are known for being cute and swinging by their tales, are native to southern Mexico.

Test Yourself – Questions

1. The Mexican flag features a snake and a(n):

    a. Bear
    b. Eagle
    c. Seal

2. The lowest point in Mexico is?

    a. Marina del Rey
    b. Mexico City
    c. Laguna Salada

3. The Trans-Mexican Volcanic Belt is known more commonly as?

    a. Rocky Mountains
    b. Sierra Nevada
    c. Sierra Oriental

4. What year did Mexico City get hit with its most devastating earthquake?

    a. 1555
    b. 2015
    c. 1985

5. Which one of these Mexican states does *not* border the United States?

    a. Chiapas
    b. Baja California
    c. Sonora

Answers

1. b
2. c
3. b
4. c
5. a

CHAPTER FOUR

MEXICAN POP CULTURE, SPORTS, AND OTHER FUN STUFF!

Unless you've visited Mexico, you've probably never really thought about the Mexican film industry, sports teams, or Mexican pop culture in general. But if you're an American, you're probably more familiar with it than you think. If you remember in the last chapter, we learned that Mexico is the most populous Spanish-speaking country in the world, and Mexico City is the largest Spanish-speaking city. As a result of its large population, Mexico sets a lot of trends in film, television, sports, and consumer goods across Latin America; its influence even extends to Spain. Also, because of Mexico's close proximity to the United States and the fact that citizens from both countries travel back and forth, many of those trends and influences make it into American society too—although they aren't always so obvious. So, continue reading to find out some things that may surprise you about Mexican sports, leisure, and pop culture.

Mexico City Is the Heart of Latin America's Film Industry

Mexico City is the number one producer of films in Latin America, which makes it the Latin American equivalent of Hollywood, although most Mexicans would scoff at that comparison. Mexico has had its own film industry since the early twentieth century and, despite a lull in the 1960s and '70s, it dominates the theaters south of the Rio Grande and even does well in Spain.

What, then, makes a Mexican film?

Films in Mexico are made just as they are anywhere else, and Mexican films span all genres. But most Latin American films in general, and Mexican films specifically, tend to be romantic comedies or dramas.

Though more and more Mexican films are making their way north of the border, prominent Mexican actors, directors, and producers have been working in the United States for years. Here are some you might not have known about.

Actor Anthony Quinn Was Born in Mexico

You might not know it based on his name, but legendary Hollywood actor Anthony Quinn was born in Mexico and was a Mexican citizen. Quinn was born in 1915, in the Mexican state of Chihuahua, to a Mexican mother named Manuela and an Irish immigrant father named Frank Quinn—which is how he got the Irish name! Frank Quinn was a bit of an adventurer, which is what brought him to Mexico, where he supposedly fought alongside Pancho Villa in the Mexican Revolution.

Frank Quinn eventually met and married Anthony's mother and then moved the family to the United States. Although Anthony lived in the U.S. for most of his life, he never forgot his Mexican roots.

During his sixty-plus-year Hollywood career, Quinn played a wide range of roles, many of them "ethnic" characters. For instance, he played Seminole Indian chief Osceola in the 1953 film *Seminole* and the Hun chieftain, Attila the Hun, in the 1954 film *Attila.* Quinn was critically praised for his ability to play both "good" and "bad" guys, exhibiting a level of depth not often seen in early films.

Quinn continued acting up until his death in 2001. The residents of his home state of Chihuahua built a statue in his honor; the sculpture portrays him doing a dance from his 1964 film *Zorba the Greek.*

Mr. Roarke from *Fantasy Island* Was Born and Worked in Mexico

If you grew up in the 1980s in America, there is a good chance that you watched *Fantasy Island*. You'll remember the mysterious Mr. Roarke who, along with his diminutive assistant Tattoo, granted fantastic wishes to guests on his island and taught them life lessons in the process. If you watched the show, then you probably know that Mr. Roarke was played by Mexican-born actor Ricardo Montalbán.

If you're a sci-fi nerd like me, then you might remember Montalbán better from his role as cosmic dictator Khan in the 1960s *Star Trek* television series and in the 1982 film *Star Trek: The Wrath of Khan*.

But Ricardo Montalbán's acting career extended far beyond these two popular roles.

Montalbán was born in 1920 in Mexico City to Spanish immigrant parents. Like Anthony Quinn, Montalbán moved to the United States with his family, which is where he spent his teen years. He then spent the 1940s traveling back and forth between Mexico and the United States, acting in films in both countries. Known for his good looks, charm, good English skills, and an exotic accent, Montalbán was able to land countless roles in American film and television from the 1950s through 1970s, often as an "ethnic" character.

If you watch enough reruns of *Bonanza, The Wild Wild West, Riverboat*, or a host of other similar shows from that era, you'll eventually see Montalbán on screen, playing either an Indian, or a bandido, or maybe even a sophisticated European out of place on the American frontier.

By the late 1970s, Montalbán had established himself well enough to land the lead role on *Fantasy Island*, and he continued to act long after that show was over. Montalbán's final credited role was in a 2009 episode of the animated television show *American Dad!*

Actress Salma Hayek Was Born and Raised in Mexico

Although her last name doesn't sound very Spanish, famous actress Salma Hayek was born and raised in the state of Veracruz and considers herself very Mexican. Hayek's father was a wealthy oil executive of Lebanese descent (hence, the non-Spanish-sounding name), and her mother is of Spanish descent.

Hayek's trademark good looks landed her roles in Mexican telenovelas (we'll get to those in a little bit) during the early 1990s, when she was in her twenties. More than just a pretty face, however, Hayek displayed great range in her acting as well as fluency in English. These qualities allowed her to make the leap to Hollywood in the mid-1990s.

Though Hayek usually plays Latina characters in American films, her looks have also enabled her to play Iranian and even Anglo-American characters. But among all the roles Hayek has played, perhaps her most critically acclaimed was as Mexican painter Frida Kahlo (1907-1954) in the 2002 film *Frida*.

What Are Telenovelas?

There's a good chance you've heard of telenovelas before.. Even if you don't know what they are, you've probably seen them lampooned and parodied on American television. Simply put, a telenovela is a Spanish-language soap opera that is in production for a very limited period of time. Unlike American soap operas, which can run for years or even decades, Latin American telenovelas are written and produced with a finite lifespan, usually about one year. The term is a combination of two words—television and novel—which indicates that, like a book, these shows have a definite beginning and end.

The first Mexican telenovelas hit the air in 1951, and just as it is with filmmaking, Mexico has become the center of Latin America's telenovela industry. Most of the top Mexican actors, such as Salma Hayek, got their start in telenovelas; actors from other Spanish-speaking countries, such as Argentina and Spain, also often hone their skills on Mexican telenovelas.

To most people outside of Latin America, Mexican telenovelas might seem a little campy, which is partly why they get parodied on American television. The acting can be a little overdramatic and the plots are often formulaic to the point of being predictable—a young couple falls in love, but different elements conspire to keep them apart.

There is also usually a stereotypical villain who tries to get the girl; this part of the story often climaxes during a wedding scene.

Telenovelas may be difficult for those who live outside of Latin America to follow, but in Mexico they are the most popular, and important type, of television show.

Erik Estrada Starred in a Hit Mexican Telenovela

Some of you may remember Erik Estrada as Officer Frank "Ponch" Poncharello in the hit American television show *CHiPs* in the late 1970s and early '80s. If you missed him in that then you might not know who I'm talking about. After the hit show, the American-born actor had problems landing another big gig and was mainly relegated to supporting roles, commercials, and "B" films.

But then there was *Dos Mujeres, un Camino.*

Dos Mujeres, un Camino was a hit Mexican telenovela that ran in 1993 and 1994. Estrada played the lead role of a hardworking Mexican truck driver who was torn between his beautiful and loyal wife, and a young waitress he met on the road. The show had all of the typical telenovela elements: occasionally melodramatic acting, a love triangle, and a villain who tried to foil the hero. The show was a huge hit in Mexico and later became a hit in other Spanish-speaking countries, making it Estrada's most successful project since *CHiPs*.

The success of *Dos Mujeres, un Camino* is not so much a testament to Estrada's acting abilities, as it is a testament to the successful medium of Mexican telenovelas across Latin America. Estrada isn't actually Mexican or even Mexican-American, but Puerto Rican. Still, when his acting career stalled he knew that he had the prerequisites to jump-start it in Mexico—good looks, name recognition, and fluency in Spanish.

Estrada may be the best-known American to try his hand in Mexican telenovelas, but thousands of others from the Spanish-speaking world also go to Mexico City every year to see if they can land a coveted role on one of the shows.

What's with Those Mexican Weather Girls?

As you read the title of this entry, you probably took a step back and maybe asked yourself a couple of questions. "Who still uses the term 'weather girls'? Is it even acceptable to say 'weather girls'? Are 'weather girls' really a thing?"

Well, in Mexico they really are a thing, and they are one of the main draws for getting people to watch the local news.

The women who deliver the weather in Mexico are extremely beautiful, usually quite curvy, and they almost always wear dresses that accentuate those curves and often show a little cleavage.

And yes, they are called "weather girls."

Clearly, the standards of what is considered sexist and what is considered acceptable for women is quite different in Mexico than it is in the U.S., which is okay for most of the Mexican weather girls, like Yanet Garcia. Garcia does the weather for Televisia Monterrey, and on the side she shows her assets on her Instagram account.

Garcia has helped bring the Mexican weathergirl phenomenon north of the border and beyond, picking up many followers in the U.S., Canada, Europe, and Asia, most of them being men!

And Mexican television executives make no apologies for promoting the beautiful weather girl trend, admitting that it is part of their strategy to attract viewers.

"We owe it to our viewers and also to our sponsors," said Televisa Monterrey weather department head

Mauro Morales. "Obviously, if a sponsor has a beautiful woman the product is going to have a greater impact. And this is of great benefit for everyone."

It is certainly of benefit to all of Yanet Garcia's fans!

Mexico's Folk Music

If you've ever been to a Mexican restaurant, in any country in the world, you've no doubt heard the Mexican traditional musical style known as *mariachi*. Mariachi music blends acoustic guitars, horns, and accordions with vocals to create a style of music that is instantly recognizable and uniquely Mexican. Over the last few decades, mariachi music has spread throughout the world and is as popular as salsa and other Latin American musical styles.

But mariachi came from fairly humble beginnings.

The precise origins of mariachi (both the music and its name), remain open to debate. But most believe that it began in the 1700s in the rural areas of the state of Jalisco. The style itself has evolved many times since then, adding new instruments and influences, as well as new clothing styles and looks.

The music originally came from mestizo peasants and, just like the people's background, the music blended elements of indigenous and European music. By the late 1800s, mariachi came to be much as it is today, with an emphasis on accordions and ballads.

The mariachi clothing style also evolved during that period.

You've probably noticed that mariachis wear very distinct styles of clothing, right? Well, these are known as charro/charra (male or female) outfits. A charro is a horse rider, similar to a cowboy in the United States, and they are very much a part of Mexican culture and history, especially in the rural areas of the northern and central states. Since mariachis originated in rural areas, and that is where the majority of their fans initially were, they adopted the charro clothing style.

They also adopted much of the charro subject matter in their lyrics.

Many of the older mariachi songs concern fighting, drinking, womanizing, and more. For most of its history, mariachi has certainly been a male-dominated musical style. But in recent years, more mariachi groups have been gender mixed and there are even some all-female mariachi bands.

Narcocorrido

Mariachi may be the best-known Mexican musical export, but it definitely not the only one. Beginning in the 1800s, a musical style known as *corrido*, or narrative ballad, became quite popular in Mexico; it peaked in the period during and after the Mexican Revolution. The lyrics of corridos often glamorized revolutionaries and the idea of the anti-hero, while the musical style was similar to mariachi with heavy emphasis on horns and accordions.

As the corrido style began to fade in popularity, it also evolved and became darker. Songs about smuggling became more frequent and, by the late 1980s, a definite subgenre emerged known as *narcocorrido*, or "drug ballad." Instead of glamorizing revolutionaries, narcocorridos glorify drug dealers, smugglers, and kingpins. As the drug war in Mexico intensified in the 2000s, the number of narcocorrido musicians also multiplied.

Even popular and legitimate musicians were willing to cash in on the lucrative drug trade.

All narcocorridos glorify the drug trade to some extent. Some even revel in the extreme violence, putting to shame lyrics you'll find in some of the most hardcore rap or heavy metal songs.

But playing narcocorrido can come with a price to the performers.

Mexican radio stations usually refuse to play known narcocorrido musicians and American stations are now following suit as they learn more about the genre. Performers still have the Internet, and the more savvy of the musicians often change their identities in order to keep playing.

And there are also problems with the cartels.

Although most of the narcocorrido musicians are not directly involved in the drug trade, many have been murdered, presumably by cartel hit men. Many narcocorrido performers glorify particular cartels, which other cartels will see as an affront. And at the other end of the spectrum, there are musicians who will diss particular kingpins in their songs.

Despite the violence associated with the genre, narcocorrido has grown in popularity in Mexico and throughout Latin America and the United States.

Toro Toro!

One of the more controversial aspects of Mexican culture is their love of bullfights. Bullfighting originated in Spain in the Middle Ages and was brought to New Spain/Mexico in the 1500s. The Mexican style of bullfighting follows the Spanish model, which incorporates several stages using many different toreadors.

European progressive sensibilities have led to bullfighting being banned in many places in Spain, so the sport's epicenter is now in Mexico.

Although bullfighting has been banned in a few Mexican states, and there are groups organized to oppose the sport, most Mexicans are either ambivalent toward it or enthusiastically support it as part of their cultural heritage. And there is no doubt that a sizable segment of Mexican society loves bullfighting—most of the world's top professional bullfighters are Mexican, and Mexico has the most bullfighting stadiums.

The largest bullfighting stadium of all is the Plaza de Toros Mexico (Stadium of Mexican Bulls) in Mexico City. The stadium opened in 1946 with a seating capacity of nearly forty-two thousand people. Although the facility is now quite dated compared to Mexico's newer soccer stadiums, large crowds still fill the rafters to cheer on their favorite bullfighters, and of course the bulls, shouting "Toro Toro!"

Soccer Is Mexico's Most Popular Sport

Soccer (or football, as Mexicans and most of the rest of the world call it) is the most popular sport in Mexico. The sport was brought to Mexico by Europeans in the 1800s, and it quickly became the most popular sport in most parts of the country. By the middle of the twentieth century, professional leagues had formed and there were several nice stadiums.

Many of the stadiums were so nice that Mexico was awarded the 1970 FIFA World Cup. The 1970 World Cup was the first one held in North America, and although Mexico didn't place in the top four, the event was viewed as a success—so much so that Mexico was awarded the World Cup again in 1986.

The Mexican professional leagues turn out a fair amount of players who go on to play for the national team, and some of the best players use the league as a stepping stone to get into the more lucrative Euro leagues. The Guadalajara team, most commonly known as Chivas, is one of the most successful and popular Mexican club teams. Chivas has won twelve league titles and has a legion of fans in Mexico and the United States.

Baseball Is a Close Second

Not far behind soccer in overall popularity in Mexico is baseball. In fact, baseball is the most popular sport in the states of Sinaloa and Sonora, which both (not coincidentally) happen to border the United States. Baseball is believed to have come to Mexico in the mid-1800s from the United States, and it has since developed alongside the older leagues north of the border, with similar rules and gameplay.

Mexico has two major professional baseball leagues: the Mexican Baseball League and the Mexican Pacific League. Although the Mexican Baseball League is older and has more teams than the Mexican Pacific League (sixteen versus ten), the Pacific League is considered the premier league because it plays in the winter.

Why would that be?

Well, since the Mexican Baseball League plays in the summer it is technically in competition with the U.S. Major League Baseball. Some major leaguers, especially Mexican nationals, play part of the season in the Pacific League.

Mexico has sent plenty of players to MLB and there are currently plenty in the league, but perhaps the best known and most successful Mexican baseball player is pitcher Fernando Valenzuela. "Fernando," as baseball fans affectionately called him, spent nearly twenty years in the MLB, mainly with the Los Angeles Dodgers. During that time (1980 to 1997), he won the prestigious Cy Young Award, the Rookie of the Year Award, and a World Series ring. He currently holds the all-time record as the Mexican National League pitcher with the most wins (173).

The Stadium Wave Was Made World Famous in Mexico

Chances are, if you've been to a packed professional (or college) sporting event, you've seen a stadium wave. If you haven't, it's when a section of the stadium's spectators stand up and sit down in unison and then the neighboring sections follow suit, creating the appearance of a human wave surging through the stadium. Some waves can go through a

113

stadium multiple times and occasionally there are opposing waves.

They definitely make the fan experience more fun and interesting.

The origins of the fan wave are a little obscure, but most believe it started in Canada or the United States in the 1970s. By the early '80s, the wave was occurring in the NHL, NFL, NBA, and MLB games as well as at college sporting events in the U.S. and minor league hockey games in Canada. By the mid-1980s, the wave had migrated south of the Rio Grande and was being done at soccer and baseball games.

And during 1986, Mexico introduced the world to the stadium wave during the World Cup.

Although the stadium wave may have started north of the Rio Grande, after the 1986 World Cup, it became known as the "Mexican Wave" in English-speaking countries outside of North America.

Today, the stadium wave is done at Australian rules football games in Australia, rugby games in New Zealand, and even tennis matches in England, where the locals all refer to it affectionately as the "Mexican Wave."

Tequila Is Named for a Town in Mexico

Yes, there is an actual town in Mexico called Tequila, which is where the distilled alcoholic beverage was first made. Tequila is a medium-sized town in the central Mexican state of Jalisco, about forty miles from the larger city of Guadalajara.

Tequila was "invented" in the late 1500s by Spanish conquistadors when they ran out of their own distilled drinks from Europe. When they saw the Aztecs and other indigenous people drinking the alcoholic drink pulque (remember that from chapter one?), they learned that it was a drink made from fermented agave plants. Pulque was more like wine or beer in strength, so the Spaniards decided to make it stronger through the distillation process.

By the early 1600s, the drink became the first alcohol to be distilled in North America, and it was produced on a mass scale when the king of Spain gave the Cuervo family a license to produce it. Eventually, other companies began distilling tequila, but the Mexican government still strictly enforces what can be labelled tequila—only a few companies outside of Jalisco are allowed to call their drink tequila. Most other drinks distilled from agave plants are known as mezcal.

Mexican exports of tequila, mezcal, and beer (such as Dos Equis) have dramatically increased in recent years, with most going to the United States. That is good news for the Mexican economy, of course. But it also happens to benefit the U.S. Trade agreements between the U.S. and Mexico allow for Mexican booze to be delivered to the U.S. in bulk and then bottled in factories north of the border, giving needed jobs to Americans.

So the next time you drink a shot of tequila, just think about all the people in the town of the same name you're helping, as well as the Americans who bottled the drink for you!

RANDOM FACTS

1. Besides having much shorter runs than American soap operas, Mexican telenovelas are also shorter in episode runtime, lasting only thirty to forty-five minutes.

2. Although far behind soccer and baseball in popularity, American football/gridiron has a sizable following in Mexico. Part of the reason can be attributed to ties between the two countries, with dual citizens and people moving back and forth across the border. Also, in recent years the National Football League (NFL) has made a concerted effort to raise interest south of the border by hosting one regular season game a year at Aztec stadium.

3. Twenty native-born Mexicans have played professional football in the NFL or other American football leagues. The most famous is Tom Fears, who was born in Guadalajara to an American father and a Mexican mother. Fears was a wide receiver during the 1950s and was later inducted into the Professional Football Hall of Fame.

4. The top Mexican soccer league, Liga MX, is considered the best professional soccer league in

North America and among the best in Latin America.

5. Mexican musician Jose Cuamea (El Shaka) was one of the more notable narcocorrido singers to be murdered. He was gunned down as he drove to a gig in Sinaloa on June 26, 2010. No arrests were ever made.

6. The "worm" you've probably heard about in tequila bottles is actually something you'd find in a bottle of mezcal. By law, gusanos, which are the larvae of moths that live in agave plants, cannot be included in tequila bottles.

7. Professional wrestling is also a very popular sport in Mexico and is known as *lucha libre* (free fighting). Mexican wrestlers, luchadores, often wear masks and rely on high-flying moves over brute strength. If you ever get down to a border town be sure to check out a match!

8. Despite having two lancers on horseback and four backup fighters, bullfighters have to be in good shape to perform. Sometimes they are injured or even killed. In 2016, Rodolfo Rodriquez died from injuries suffered in a bullfight. He was the longest active bullfighter in Mexico, dying at the age of sixty-four!

9. Ranchera is another popular style of Mexican music. Like other forms discussed in this chapter,

it originated in the rural areas of the country, which is signified by its name "ranch."

10. The city of Guadalajara has hosted an international film festival every year since 1986. More than three hundred films have been screened there, and it has become very popular with Spanish-speaking actors, directors, writers, and producers from around the world.

11. Unlike the United States, Mexico doesn't have much of an adult film industry, although pornography is generally legal in Mexico for adults to produce and consume.

12. Academy Award winning-director Guillermo del Toro Gomez was born and raised in Guadalajara.

13. The national dance of Mexico is called the jarabe tapatio, but English speakers know it as the "Mexican hat dance." Though the dance moves were influenced by Spanish dance, they were given a distinctly Mexican twist in the 1800s, namely with a male and female dancing around a sombrero.

14. Corona, which is brewed by Grupo Modelo, is the best-selling Mexican beer. The light lager is popular worldwide and is usually in the top five of most consumed.

15. Although the main event of the Mexican bullfight closely resembles its Spanish ancestor in terms of

rules, the event itself is uniquely Mexican. Along with the fights, spectators are treated to Mexican folk dances and rodeo events that are more American than European.

16. *Folklorico* is the name for all traditional or folk Mexican dances, which includes the Mexican hat dance. The bright costumes of the dancers, especially the women, are often unique to their state of origin.

17. Boxing is probably the most popular non-team sport in Mexico. Mexico has produced many champions in the light and middleweights, most notably Julio Ceasar Chavez, who amassed a 107-6-2 record with an incredible eighty-six knockouts! Chavez held multiple belts during the 1980s and '90s.

18. Soviet film director Sergei Eisenstein visited Mexico in the 1930s and produced *Que Viva Mexico*. Although the film was not a major hit, it is said that it inspired Mexican directors, producers, and writers to examine deeper ideas in film.

19. The Mexican national team plays in the Confederation of North, Central American and Caribbean Association Football (CONCACAF) for FIFA competitions. Mexico has dominated play in the federation since it began in 1961.

20. Hugo Sanchez is universally regarded as the best Mexican soccer player of all time. He played over twenty years, primarily in Spain, and later managed club teams in Mexico and the Mexican national team.

Test Yourself – Questions

1. A telenovela is a:

   a. A movie
   b. A commercial
   c. A television show

2. Actress Salma Hayek was born and raised in:

   a. Mexico City
   b. Sonora
   c. Veracruz

3. This is considered the top professional baseball league in Mexico:

   a. Mexican Pacific League
   b. Mexico City League
   c. Sonora Baseball League

4. This is the world's largest bullfighting ring/stadium:

   a. Plaza de Sonora
   b. Plaza de Toros Mexico
   c. Aztec Stadium

5. What is the name of the type of song that glorifies drug smuggling and cartels?

   a. Narcocorrido
   b. Narco Rap
   c. Narco Metal

Answers

1. c
2. c
3. a
4. b
5. a

CHAPTER FIVE

VISTING MEXICO

Now that you know as much as anybody about Mexico's history, geography, and popular culture, it's time to plan your trip. In this next chapter we'll look at some of the best places to visit (we've already met a few in the previous chapter) and also a couple to avoid. You'll find out where the best beaches are for casual tourists, as well as where some of the more remote ones are for those of you hankering for adventure. We'll also talk about some of the national parks, the best archaeological sites open to the public, and some of Mexico's best museums.

Cruising Is a Good Option

If you don't know Spanish and haven't traveled very much, you might want to consider a cruise as a good way to see Mexico. Cruise ships bring guests to generally safe, if not crowded, ports of Mexico. Don't worry, cruise ships aren't full of retirees—unless you happen to get on a cruise that is meant for retirees — and can be an affordable and fun way to travel.

Several different cruise liners offer trips to Mexico of varying prices for trips that last anywhere from two days to more than a week. Most of the cruise ships depart from the ports of Los Angeles, New Orleans, or Miami, depending on where your trip is going.

If you sail out of Los Angeles, you can see the sights of Baja California and Baja California Sur, such as Ensenada and Puerto Chiapas.

If you want to see Mexico's Gulf and/or Caribbean coasts, then you'll have to sail out of either New Orleans, Miami (or other Florida ports), or Texas. These trips tend to be a little longer, but there is usually much more to see. Besides docking in resort towns, Caribbean ships often stop at, or near, Mayan sites such as Chichen Itza. Some Caribbean cruises also offer daily excursions into the rain forests of the Yucatan.

There is no doubt that you'll see a lot of Mexico very quickly on a cruise, but if you want to see the details you'll have to do so on your own.

The National Museum of Anthropology

Mexico's largest, most visited, and arguably best museum is the Museo Nacional de Anthropolgia, or National Museum of Anthropology. Located in the center of Mexico City in Chapultepec Park, the museum boasts of one of the largest and best curated collections of pre-Columbian art and artifacts in the world.

The museum began through a combination of private donations in the 1800s and grew in the 1900s, as Mexican nationalism combined with new scientific archaeological methods. Artifacts discovered at archaeological sites around Mexico, from all periods, began to be exhibited in the museum. By the early 1960s, the museum had outgrown its home, so a new, larger museum was built. The post-modern building where the collection in now housed contains twenty-three rooms that feature all periods of Mexico's pre-Columbian history—Olmecs, Mayans, Toltecs, and other cultures—but there is no question that the Aztecs are the main attraction at this museum.

You'll see murals, statues, jewelry, and other artifacts used by the people of Mexico before the Spanish arrived. But the item that receives the most views is the Aztec Sun Stone.

The wheel-shaped Aztec calendar has a one hundred forty-one-inch diameter and is thirty-nine inches thick. The calendar was discovered in 1790 and is believed to have been created just before the Spanish arrived.

The Sun Stone is one of the best-preserved examples of the complex way in which Mesoamerican peoples viewed time. The calendar has three rings that represent different cycles of time—remember reading about that earlier in this book?

Many of Mexico's Archaeological Sites Are Major Attractions

Every year, hundreds of thousands of people visit Mexico's many pre-Columbian sites. And now that you now about Mexico's history, you'll know which ones are the coolest! Although there are close to thirty thousand archaeological sites in Mexico, the vast majority are off-limits to the public. Some are in inaccessible places, while others are currently being worked on by scholars. And some are little more than a monument or two.

Still, there are nearly two hundred sites you can see, so if doing a little hiking up a pyramid is your thing, you have plenty of options. All of the sites are cared for by the government and the most popular ones have plenty of facilities and vendors available for hungry, thirsty, and intrepid explorers.

If you're staying in Mexico City, you have plenty of options, beginning with the site of Teotihuacán. If you remember back to chapter one, Teotihuacán was the capital of an empire in the Central Mexican Valley in the first few centuries AD and is only about thirty miles southwest of Mexico City. The site is well-preserved, and visitors can walk up and down many of the temples, just as human sacrifice victims did!

Well, they didn't actually get to walk back down, did they?

Also just a short trip from Mexico City is the Toltec capital of Tula. You can either go from Teotihuacán to Tula, or from Mexico City to Tula; both are short car or bus rides. Since Tula is on the other end of Mexico City, many people divide the two sites into two different trips. Once at Tula, you'll be impressed by the preserved colossal statues that stand guard over the area just as they did one thousand years ago.

Another one of the most popular archaeological sites—but a bit more out of the way—is Chichen Itza. If you'll remember back to chapter one, Chichen Itza was a major Mayan city, complete with an impressive pyramid, ball court, and astronomical observatory. Although Chichen Itza is in the Yucatan and quite far from Mexico City, it is connected to the city of Cancun by a four-lane tollway. Many cruise ships also offer day trips to Chichen Itza.

Of course, there are many more sites that a more curious traveler can find if he or she wants to avoid the crowds.

The National Museum of History Is Also Great

Located in the same neighborhood as the National Museum of Anthropology is the Museo Nacional de Historia, or Museum of National History. The building that houses the museum's pieces is quite an impressive architectural example and also a piece of history in itself.

It is the Chapultepec Castle, remember that?

Yes, that's right! It was the final defense point the Mexicans held in the Mexican-American War before it was stormed by the Americans, who went on to win the war. You'll find artifacts from that war, as well as items dating from the arrival of the Spanish and beyond.

Every year, more than two million visitors come to the museum to learn about Pancho Villa and the Mexican Revolution, Mexico's time as New Spain, and to see rooms that the Emperor Maximillian I and his wife lived in while they briefly ruled Mexico in the 1800s.

Located on the top of a hill, the museum is definitely a landmark in central Mexico City.

Mexico City's Central Park

New York City has Central Park, but Mexico City is home to the equally impressive (and nearly as large) Bosque de Chapultepec, or "Chapultepec Forrest."

The forest is often referred to simply as Chapultepec Park, or Chapultepec.

Chapultepec is one of the most visited urban parks in the world, and it is also one of the largest at over seventeen hundred acres. The park has quite an interesting history, as it was first a retreat for Aztec rulers before it became the site of the Chapultepec Castle. During the 1960s, the city expanded the park into three sections.

Just like parks in other major cities around the world, Chapultepec has running paths, small lakes that are the remnants of Lake Texcoco, and cultural attractions. Besides being located right below Chapultepec Castle, the park grounds in section one also house the National Museum of Anthropology.

Surf's Up, Bro!

You might not think of Mexico as a surfing mecca, but located up and down its Pacific coast are hundreds of beaches, of varying sizes, where surfers from all over come to ride the sweet Mexican waves. Mazatlán in Sinaloa, Sayulita in Nayarit, Cuyutlán in Colima, and Trocones in Guerro all have some primo waves, but none of them beat Ensenada in Baja California.

Located just seventy-eight miles from San Diego, Ensenada is a major tourist destination and easily reached via a four-lane toll highway. Many Americans work and live in Ensenada, so making your way around this city of about two hundred seventy thousand people is much easier than in other parts of Mexico.

And there is no doubt that Ensenada's main tourist draw is its beaches, and many of those beaches are known for their sweet waves. Ensenada's main surfing beaches are San Miguel Beach, California Trailer Park, Stacks, and the 3 M's, which attract surfers from the States, Brazil, Australia, Chile, and all points in between. Because the waves in Ensenada are so tubular, and because costs are much cheaper, these beaches are the sites of many professional surfing competitions.

If you've never surfed but are interested in learning, don't worry. There are many surf shops along the beaches that offer lessons from friendly, professional surfers.

Mexico Has Plenty of National Parks

Sixty-seven to be exact, located in twenty-three of Mexico's thirty-one states, which means that if you visit Mexico you'll be near one. With that said, not all of Mexico's national parks are created equally, with some having better facilities and accessibility than others. There is something for everyone in Mexico's national parks: Some are located on beautiful beaches, while others are in mountainous terrain, and some are located in the rain forests and jungles of southern Mexico.

Mexico's largest national park is Arrecife Alacranes National Park, also known as Scorpion Reef. As the name suggests, it is actually a collection of five small islands off the Yucatan Peninsula that covers more than two thousand square miles of area. Scorpion Reef is known for its snorkeling, deep sea diving, fishing, and bird-watching.

If you plan on visiting Scorpion Reef, lodging and provisions are available on the mainland.

If you're staying in Mexico City and want to take a break from the archaeological sites to get back to nature, then Cumbres del Ajusco National Park may be a good option. Located just outside of Mexico City, this park offers alpine hiking opportunities that rival central Europe and the American Rockies.

Most of Mexico's larger and more popular national parks have modern lodging and facilities, so you won't have to ditch your cell phone or laptop to get back to nature!

The Lacandon Jungle

If you prefer rain forests to beaches or mountains, then the Lacandon Jungle is the place to visit. Located in the state of Chiapas' border with Guatemala, the jungle covers more than ten thousand acres of land, including tropical trees, rivers, lakes, monkeys, and jaguars. The Montes Azules Biosphere Reserve was created in 1978 in a section of Chiapas because of the biodiversity of the jungle. Conservationists want to preserve the jungle's delicate ecosystem from deforestation, poaching, and pollution.

Although the Lacandon Jungle is quite remote, adventuresome explorers can arrange guided tours into the rain forest from the largest city in Chiapas, Tuxtal Gutierrez.

If you venture into the Lacandon jungle though, it's not all just trees and monkeys. Some of the best preserved Mayan sites are also in the rain forest, including: Palenque, Bonampak, and Chinkultic. If nothing else, seeing the well-preserved murals from one of the temples alone is worth the trip.

The King of All Resort Towns

Without a doubt, there is no question that Acapulco is the king of Mexican resort cities. Or, at least, it once was. Beginning in the middle of the twentieth century, wealthy Americans began regularly visiting Acapulco's sunny beaches and, before too long, a major tourist industry popped up in the state of Guerrero's largest city. American and European tourists came for the pristine beaches and nearby pre-Columbian sites, and American cruise ships made it a regular stop in their itineraries.

High-rise resorts began popping up in the 1960s and large nightclubs followed. The tourist industry certainly provided many jobs and stimulated the local economy.

But by the late 2000s, the good times had largely come to an end.

A combination of poverty and Mexico's drug war adversely affected life in Acapulco for Mexicans and all but killed the tourist industry. The drug cartels began using Guerrero as a major smuggling area, and as they did so violence increased. There were nine hundred forty-eight homicides in Acapulco in 2018, which put it at number two in per capita homicides, just behind Tijuana, Mexico.

Although the violence has generally not spilled over into the resort areas, the reputation of it, combined with the economic recession in the late 2000s, was enough to drive some of the resorts out of business.

But as dangerous as Acapulco may be, it probably isn't at the top of most people's list of locales to avoid.

You Should Probably Avoid These Places in Mexico

As dangerous and lawless as Acapulco has become, you are still pretty safe if you stay in the resorts. There are some cities (and even states) in Mexico, however, that you should consider avoiding altogether.

Because of the cartel wars, many of the border states—Sonora, Chihuahua, and Tamaulipas, in particular—are extremely dangerous and probably should be avoided. The states of Sinaloa, Jalisco, and Nuevo Leon are also to be avoided. The U.S. State Department has issued travel advisories for most of these states. Victoria, Tamaulipas, Juarez, Chihuahua, and Culiacan, Sinaloa are among the world's most dangerous cities per capita. Although much of the truly horrendous crime in these states is narco driven, and directed at either warring cartels or the police and military, there is also a considerable amount of random crime in the urban areas.

Apart from the coastal areas in these states, which have resorts, there is little reason for outsiders to visit these places. If you don't know Spanish, you'll stick out like a sore thumb and look like a "mark." And even if you do speak the language, if you don't know locals or have legitimate business in the area, there's really no reason to visit.

Although the U.S-Mexican border has become a dangerous and lawless place, Americans are still drawn to the number one border town—Tijuana.

If You're Careful, Tijuana Is Worth Visiting

Just across the international border from San Diego, California is Mexico's sixth most populous city and the largest city in Baja California, Tijuana. You've probably heard stories about Tijuana being a place where prostitution is common, illicit drugs are plentiful, and you can even pay to watch, well, some pretty crazy things involving people and animals. You've also probably heard that you can very easily get robbed or have your throat cut as you do those things.

All of that is still true about Tijuana—there is a seedy red-light district, crime is common in some areas, and it is (per capita) the most dangerous city in the world. With that said, the city has made legitimate strides in recent years to repair its reputation. There is a heavy police presence in many of the tourist areas, and if you find yourself in trouble, chances are you were looking for it.

More than three hundred thousand tourists cross the border into Tijuana every day, most of them looking for some good Baja Mexican food and possibly some good deals at the many markets. Just about everything is cheaper in Tijuana than it is north of the border, including prescription drugs. If you're doing a little shopping, be sure to get a picture with a Tijuana zebra—it's just a donkey painted to look like a zebra.

They don't have the same animal rights laws south of the border.

Tijuana also doesn't have the same laws regarding prostitution. Many tourists still come to Tijuana for prostitution. A lot of robberies and other criminal activities also take place in the red-light district.

You should also be aware of being shaken down by the Tijuana police, who are known for being notoriously corrupt.

Cabo Wabo

As Acapulco and some of the other, older Mexican resort towns began losing popularity due to crime and other factors in the 1990s, the once sleepy town of Cabo San Lucas was there to pick up the slack. Located at the very end of the Baja Peninsula in the state of Baja California Sur, Cabo San Lucas, along with neighboring city San Jose del Cabo, has become the premier resort destination in Mexico. Made famous by American rocker Sammy Haggar in the 1990s, who opened a nightclub in the city named "Cabo Wabo" after one of his songs, the city boasts of beautiful beaches, nice weather, and friendly people.

Cabo San Lucas has become a popular destination for scuba divers and is a common stop for cruise ships. If you go diving or snorkeling, you'll need to check out El Arco, or "The Arch of Cabo San Lucas." This arch is a natural rock formation off the tip of the Baja, marking the dividing line between the Pacific Ocean and the Gulf of California.

The seas off Cabo are also known for excellent fishing, luring anglers from all over to fish for mahi-mahi and marlin.

Aztec Stadium Is More Than a Mile High

The fans of the NFL team the Denver Broncos like to take pride in their stadium, Mile High Stadium, and the supposed advantage the high elevation brings their team. But it is nothing compared to Estadio Azteca (Aztec Stadium) in Mexico City.

The world famous Aztec Stadium is seventy-two hundred feet above sea level, which makes it almost two thousand feet higher than Mile High Stadium! The high altitude stadium opened in 1966 as a multiuse stadium, but has mostly served as a soccer stadium. It was the primary stadium when Mexico hosted the 1970 and 1986 World Cups and it is the home for Cruz Azul and Club América of the first tier Mexican soccer league, Liga MX.

If you catch a game at Aztec Stadium, you'll be rubbing elbows with up to ninety-five thousand other fans, as the stadium is the largest in Mexico and the ninth largest in North America.

But Aztec Stadium doesn't host just soccer games.

Since 1994, the stadium has regularly hosted one regular season NFL game, although the American players are never too crazy about playing at such a high elevation.

Although located about twelve miles from central Mexico City in a residential area, Aztec Stadium is easy to get to via the light rail line. Once there, don't expect to get hot dogs or nachos in the stadium (no, nachos aren't Mexican fare). Instead, you can load up on quesadillas and burritos.

Hey, that sounds good to me!

Hitting the Markets

One final thing you certainly have to do if you're in Mexico City is to hit one of its many and affordable public markets. Yes, Mexico City has modern shopping malls and other retail "box stores," but if you really want to get an authentic feel for the city and the country you need to visit some of the markets.

Mexico City's oldest, and by far largest, public market is Mercado La Merced. The market is located in central Mexico City, so finding it via public transportation is easy. All of the locals also know about it, so you only have to ask.

The market is a strange and wonderful blend of Mexico's pre-Columbian past and its place in the modern world, which is no doubt due to the age of the place. The market dates back to the 1500s, when the first Spanish in Mexico traded with the indigenous people. But it is probably much older, as the Aztecs and other people also traded in similar open-air markets.

Encompassing a four-square block area, you can find everything from furniture to electronics in the market. But for many tourists, the draw is the exotic foods and spices. You can buy edible cactus, corn fungus, and even edible bugs! Yes, some bugs are a delicacy in Mexico.

So bring your appetite, some pesos, and be ready to haggle with the vendors.

RANDOM FACTS

1. President Adolfo Lopez Mateos was a major advocate of the arts and Mexican culture during his presidency from 1958 through 1964. During his office, the National Museum of Anthropology and the Museum of Modern Art were opened, along with several smaller museums.

2. Sammy Haggar developed the term "Cabo Wabo" by taking the nickname for Cabo San Lucas and combing it with a shortened version of "wobble." The wobble/wabo, of course, refers to how intoxicated many tourists get when they visit the city.

3. The people of the Lacandon Jungle are primarily indigenous, with many of them speaking Mayan languages.

4. Aztec Stadium was the scene of two of the most famous events in soccer history. The first was the "Game of the Century" between Italy and West Germany in the 1970 World Cup. Italy won the game 4-3. The second came during the 1986 World Cup when Argentine player Diego Maradona scored an improbable goal against several English defenders, giving Argentina a 2-1

victory over England and earning the title of "Goal of the Century."

5. In an interesting and somewhat ironic turn, as violence and crime peaked in Tijuana in the late 2000s, many of the city's elite bought expensive homes in San Diego. At the same time, many Americans began buying homes and apartments in Tijuana's more exclusive neighborhoods.

6. Some of the strange (at least to Americans) food you'll find at Mercado La Merced include a salsa made from flying ants and dried grasshoppers. The locals will assure you that they're great, so give it a try!

7. Although Mexico's best surfing waves are on its long Pacific coastline, there are some spots on the Gulf and Caribbean coastlines that are surfable. The swells aren't as big unless there is a hurricane coming, but sometimes that only attracts more surfers!

8. NFL players usually don't like playing in Mexico City. The city itself is never cited as a problem, but the elevation is just too much for some of the big guys to handle.

9. Chihuahua may be a dangerous place in general, but it is home to a beautiful natural attraction known as Copper Canyon. It is actually a collection of six canyons in the middle of the

Sierra Madre Occidental in southwestern Chihuahua.

10. In 2017, thirty-five million tourists visited Mexico, making it the eighth most popular tourist destination that year.

11. Among tourists, Americans represent the number one nationality (by far) at over ten million per year. Canadians are second, with around two million per year.

12. Mexico's Dia de Muertos (Day of the Dead) has become a major tourist attraction in recent years. (We'll talk more about its origins in the next chapter.)

13. Mexico is the number one medical tourist destination for Americans, and ranks twenty-ninth overall in the world. People go there for easy-to-get and cheaper medications, as well as nonconventional treatments.

14. The neighborhood of Coyoacan (place of coyotes) has become a popular tourist destination in recent years. The brightly painted yellow-and-red houses give the neighborhood a definite charm and uniqueness, and the numerous coffee shops, bistros, bars, and museums make it an interesting place to visit.

15. If you make it to the state of Oaxaca, be sure to check out the Hierve el Agua, also known as the

"frozen waterfall." Although it really does look like a frozen waterfall, it is actually a formation of calcium carbonate on the side of a mountain.

16. The Zócalo, which is the central square of Mexico City, is visited by eighty-five million people a year, making it the second most-visited tourist spot in the world after the Grand Bazaar in Istanbul, Turkey.

17. Located just across the Rio Grande from El Paso, Texas, Juarez was a popular party spot for young Americans until the 1990s. Since that time, the Juarez and Sinaloa cartels have engaged in a bloody war that has left thousands dead.

18. Puerto Vallarta is a popular resort city in the state of Jalisco. It has been showcased in a number of American movies and television shows.

19. Yes, iguana is a popular meal in some parts of Mexico. Iguana can be prepared in a number of different ways, including barbequed. Enthusiasts of iguana meat claim that the different colored lizards have different tastes, with green iguana being the most popular.

20. Similar to Central Park in New York, Chapultepec Park also has plenty of street vendors that are supposed to be licensed by the city. However, the city has had problems with unlicensed vendors and occasional vagrants. I guess Central Park and Chapultepec Park really do have a lot in common!

Test Yourself – Questions

1. What is Mexico's largest sports stadium?
   a. Mayan Stadium
   b. Olmec Stadium
   c. Aztec Stadium

2. This is where you'll find the largest collection of Mesoamerican artifacts in the world:
   a. International Museum of Mesoamerican Studies
   b. National Museum of Anthropology
   c. National Museum of History

3. This is the largest national park in Mexico:
   a. Volcano Grande National Park
   b. Arrecife Alacranes National Park/Scorpion Reef
   c. Mayan Ruins National Park

4. In which of these Mexican states will you find some totally tubular surfing?
   a. Baja California
   b. Tamaulipas
   c. Chiapas

5. This city was the first modern resort city in Mexico:
   a. Acapulco
   b. Juarez
   c. Reynosa

Answers

1. c
2. b
3. b
4. a
5. a

CHAPTER SIX

WEIRD MEXICO: FOLKLORE, LEGENDS, AND GHOST STORIES!

Now that you know about Mexico's long and diverse history, it's time to take a look at some of the more "popular" stories regarding Mexico's history and culture. Keep reading to learn about how mythical legends about the Aztecs' origins have turned political, how cute little Chihuahua dogs became associated with Mexico, and what role the Virgin of Guadalupe plays in modern Mexican religion and culture. You'll also be introduced to some strange and scary aspects of Mexican culture. You'll read about how the Day of the Dead holiday came about through a combination of indigenous and European traditions, and you will find the answer to some other questions: Why is a mansion in Monterrey believed to be haunted? Why are there a bunch of dolls hanging from wires on an island outside

Mexico City? Why do some drug smugglers and cartel members think different saints will protect them? All of these questions (and more) will be covered in this final chapter. But be warned, this chapter may give you goosebumps.

The Day of the Dead Is Like Halloween and All Saints' Day

Well, sort of. Actually it is a three-day festival that begins on October 31 and ends on November 2. The festival is extremely popular in central and southern Mexico, where many pre-Columbian traditions still persist. Essentially, the holiday is a celebration of deceased friends and relatives and of the Aztec goddess of the dead.

Traditionally, people's graves are decorated with flowers and fake skulls— although, at one time, the skulls were very real. There are also parades where people dress up like skeletons, especially women, who take on the identity of "La Calavera Catrina," or the "Elegant Skull Lady." La Calavera Catrina is believed to be the modern incarnation of the ancient Aztec goddess of death.

Since the celebration takes place during Halloween, and there are some scary-looking outfits associated with it, the Day of the Dead does seem a lot like Halloween.

But it clearly began as an Aztec festival, and one that the Spanish didn't like. As a result, the people began celebrating it on November 1, which coincided with All Saints' Day in Europe.

If you ever happen to end up in the middle of a Day of the Dead festival, have fun! Mexicans actually view the holiday as a happy one where they eat, drink, and remember the dead fondly.

They just happen to do it dressed up like scary-looking skeletons!

Juan Diego and the Virgin of Guadalupe

If you have any familiarity with Mexicans, then you know that they are ardent Roman Catholics. If you've been in the home of Mexicans, you've probably seen images of the Virgin Mary; you've also probably seen jewelry inspired by the Virgin Mary.

For Mexicans, it is actually Our Lady of Guadalupe, or the Virgin of Guadalupe. According to both Mexican and Roman Catholic tradition, a vision of the Virgin Mary appeared to an indigenous Mexican peasant named Juan Diego on a hill outside Mexico City on December 9, 1531.

Diego saw the vision several more times, and this vision told him that his ailing uncle would be cured of his illness. A chapel was erected on the site of the vision, along with an image of the Virgin Mary, which came to be associated with great miracles. Eventually, the Church recognized the image as holy.

The village of Guadalupe, which was where the vision was seen, eventually became a suburb of Mexico City, and the small chapel for the image became the Basilica of Our Lady of Guadalupe in Mexico City. The image of the Virgin is very distinct, as it shows her standing, praying over a cherub with a crown on her head. Gold rays surround the image.

The image has become so much a part of Mexican culture that even nonbelievers will invoke the image of the Virgin of Guadalupe as a sign of patriotism and pride in Mexican history.

The Mythical Aztec Homeland

If you remember back to chapter one, we talked about how the Aztecs originally came from what is today the American southwest, and they eventually ended up in the Central Mexican Valley. According to the Aztec legends, the name of their ancestral home was *Aztlan*. But separating the myth from reality has been difficult.

The myths state that the Aztecs were one of seven tribes that inhabited seven caves in a region known as Chicomoztoc. The tribes left Cicomoztoc after awhile and eventually settled in Aztlan, which was described as being an island.

There are several different Aztec legends about Aztlan, so locating it, (if it even existed) has proven to be difficult. Some scholars believe that Aztlan is symbolic of the place where the Aztecs began their long journey, while others think that it is purely mythical. Some who think it is myth point out its similarities to the Atlantis myth, which has led to some pretty wild and unfounded theories about a pre-flood civilization that connected the Old and New Worlds.

Still, others have used the Aztlan myth to advance political agendas. Militant Chicano groups in the United States have claimed Aztlan as the states that were taken from Mexico in the Mexican-American War, mixing and confusing ancient and modern history with current ethnic politics.

Most Mexicans in Mexico know little about the Chicano Aztlan theory, and those who do care little about it.

For most Mexicans, Aztlan is more of a concept than anything. It represents a golden age that was lost, but that can possibly be recaptured one day.

Dolls Can Be Very Creepy

Especially when there are hundreds of mutilated ones hanging from trees and pinned to doors!

Not far from Aztec Stadium, located among the canals of the Xochimilco neighborhood, is a chinampa known as the Island of the Dolls. As the name indicates, it's a very small island with hundreds of creepy dolls hanging from tree branches.

The story is that the owner of the island, Julian Santana Barrera, began hanging the dolls after a girl drowned there in the 1950s.

Barrera said that he hung them to ward off evil spirits, but anyone who has seen them will attest to how creepy and evil they look.

Over the decades, the place has become a bit of a tourist attraction. Besides the cringe factor, which makes it worth seeing for many, there is also an element of adventure in finding and getting to the place. In the years before the Internet, you had to really know where you were going to locate it, and even if you did know where to go, you had to find a boatman willing to give you a ride in his trajinera.

Perhaps ironically, Barrera himself drowned nearby in 2001.

The island was later passed on to other owners who have capitalized on its weird, creepy history. They opened a small museum in Barrera's former house where you can see his original dolls, including his favorite one, known as Agustinita. Some visitors even leave offerings for Agustinita.

Now, that's creepy!

The Piñata Has Legendary Origins

There's a good chance that you've played the piñata game at some point in your life, or if you haven't, you've seen others play it. For anyone not familiar with it, it may actually seem like a pretty strange exercise.

The player is blindfolded, given a stick, and told to hit a papier-mâché object/container that is hanging in the middle of the room. Once the container is hit well enough, or enough times, it breaks open and all sorts of candy and/or fruit falls out.

It is really pretty fun!

Today, piñatas are most commonly used at birthday parties, but they have a long and varied tradition in Mexico, which is the modern home of the activity.

The piñata tradition probably originated in Italy, where it was called *pignata* (earthenware cooking pot) and done during Lent. The pots would be filled with various edible treats and colorful ribbons and then smashed in a game similar to the modern version. From Italy, the game traveled along the Mediterranean Sea coastline to Spain, where it also became a popular Lent activity.

The Spanish then brought the tradition to Mexico in the 1500s, where the Mayans and Aztecs were also already practicing a similar tradition that was also religious in nature. Although the Aztec tradition was for their god Huitzilopochtli, the treats stored inside the pots they used were colorful flowers.

No human hearts were used for the Aztec piñatas!

As with so much of Mexican history and culture, the European and Mesoamerican traditions merged to create the modern piñata tradition. Modern Mexican Catholics often interpret the piñata in terms of religious symbolism: It is seen as a struggle against evil, and the blindfold on the participant represents his or her faith.

For most people, though, the piñata is just a fun activity to do at a birthday party.

"No Me Mates, Gabriel!"

The city of Monterrey, Nuevo Leon has experienced its fair share of problems in recent years. Crime has plagued the state and the city and dried up the barely existing tourist trade.

But there *is* one place that has drawn its fair share of visitors in the last few years.

The mansion at 1026 Jose Aramberri Street sits abandoned, unlived in with the possible exception of two otherworldly inhabitants.

You see, this house, known to locals as La Casa de Aramberri, is believed to be haunted by a woman and her daughter who were brutally murdered there in 1933. The details of the murders are quite gory and frightening, and the story becomes even more bizarre when you throw in a parrot, swift justice, and a couple of ghosts.

One day in 1933, when the owner went to work, three crooks entered the home. . They believed there was a cache of silver coins stashed in the house, and when they didn't find their treasure they turned their wrath on the women.

The mother and daughter were found by the father, both nearly decapitated.

The police began their investigation and quickly determined that there were no signs of forced entry. As they continued their search, they noticed a cute little parrot in a cage repeating some phrases he had heard. After a few minutes, the phrase caught the attention of the police: "No mae mate, Gabriel!" or "Don't kill me, Gabriel!"

It turns out that Gabriel was the nephew of the husband/father. When the police "questioned" Gabriel, it didn't take long for him to flip on his two coconspirators.

Instead of waiting for a trail, the police took the three killers out to the desert, shot them, and then brought their bodies back to Monterrey for all to see.

In the years after the murders, people tried to live in the house. But sightings of two female apparitions yelling, "No mae mate, Gabriel!" proved too much for residents to handle. The house was eventually abandoned, with only the occasional vagrant or mischievous child wandering inside.

And, of course, the murdered woman and her daughter who will apparently keep demanding for Gabriel to not kill them.

Run If You See This Ghost

If you're ever passing through the central Mexican state of Guanajuato and you end up in the sleepy little town of Jaral del Progresso, you'll find some great scenery and friendly people—but not a whole lot for a tourist to do.

You can visit Benito Juarez Park and, if you're really brave, you can try to do it at night.

According to local legends, the park was built on an old cemetery (which is bad enough), but things got creepier years later when the city decided to add some modern park benches.

It wasn't long before the park benches were getting vandalized nearly every night, so the city decided to hire a night watchman. It didn't take the watchman long to catch the culprit.

As he was doing his patrol, the watchman noticed what looked like an old woman vandalizing the park benches. When he approached her, he noticed that it was no ordinary woman—before he could react, the apparition physically attacked him. The watchman later came down with a strange illness and was replaced with another night watchman.

The second night watchman was also attacked and came down with a similar, mysterious illness.

The city has since closed the park at night, but a camera has caught an image of a nighttime park visitor that has become famous on the Internet. It is what appears to be a glowing, nearly translucent woman standing next to a tree.

Narco Saints

Now that you've come this far in the book, you know that Mexicans are generally a religious people, and you also know that they have a diverse history that mixes elements of European and Mesoamerican cultures. Furthermore, you know that crime is a big problem in some areas of Mexico, especially the drug cartel-related violence in the northern states. So what happens when you mix all of that together?

You get narco saints?

That's right, saints are patronized by cartel members for favors as they carry out their nefarious deeds. This is a thing in Mexico and it seems to be getting more popular every year.

It is believed that the first patron of narco saints was a bandido named Jesus Malverde, who lived in the late 1800s and early 1900s in Sinaloa. Whether he even lived is a matter of debate. But many of the people of Sinaloa believe he did, and those people see him as a sort of anti-hero who committed crimes for the people.

A Mexican Robin Hood if you will.

By the 1970s, a shrine was built for him in the town of Culiacan. Though it was eventually torn down, a second one was built in another section of the town. As the cartels began gaining power and prestige in the 1990s and 2000, more and more cartel members began giving offerings to Malverde's shrine and praying to him.

But Jesus Malverde is not the only narco saint.

Santa Muerte, or Saint Death, is another popular saint with the cartels, as are dozens of others that are only known in certain regions. The Catholic Church is vehemently opposed to these narco saints. But, as experts have pointed out, they tend to be a remnant of Mexico's pre-European past, where violent deities were given blood offerings for protection in battle.

Experts have also stated that the trend of narco saints will probably continue to grow as the cartels become more powerful in some areas of Tamaulipas, Sinaloa, Sonora, Chihuahua, and other northern states.

The Weeping Woman

If you're ever driving on a lonely Mexican highway in the middle of the night and see a woman on the side of the road crying, you might just want to keep going because it could be "La Llorna," or the "Weeping Woman."

The legend of La Llorna has been around Mexico for more than one hundred years and has some different versions, but all tell the tale of a tragic love affair gone wrong. La Llorna was a woman who was in love with a man, but he wasn't in love with her and didn't want to be a father to her two children. In order to make her lover happy, La Llorna drowned her two children and then told her lover that she no longer had children.

She was rejected again by her lover.

Overcome with guilt by what she had done, La Llorna drowned herself in the spot where she killed her children. She was then damned to walk the rural areas of Mexico for eternity, searching for her lost children.

They say if you listen real closely in the desert of northern Mexico on a quiet night, you can hear a weeping woman. Is it La Lorna?

Chihuahua Dogs Really Are from Chihuahua

Chihuahuas are one of the funniest dog breeds. And also the smallest. The pint-sized dogs are famous for an obstreperous and bellicose attitude that far exceeds their diminutive size.

Their breed name has also elicited a few chuckles and seems to fit them for some reason. But as funny as the name "Chihuahua" may seem to many, it really is where the breed originated.

Now that you're an expert on Mexican geography, you know that Chihuahua is a state in northern Mexico. Chihuahua is where the modern breed of dog was first recognized by organized dog breeders in the 1800s and given the name. But their history goes back possibly more than one thousand years prior.

Small statues of small dogs that resemble the Chihuahua have been found in Mesoamerican archaeological sites across Mexico. This ancient dog was known as the Techichi, which had quite an interesting history. It was favored as a pet by the Toltecs. But the Aztecs apparently preferred to eat the Techichi.

Techichi meat was apparently so popular among the Aztecs that it was quite common in their markets!

After the Spanish conquered Mexico, the Techichi

was probably bred with European dogs, resulting in the modern-day Chihuahua.

This Is the Most Haunted Cemetery in Mexico

If you go to Guadalajara, Jalisco, you might pass by the Panteon de Belan, also known as the Santa Paula Cemetery. It really isn't much to look at and has been closed since 1896, but it still draws plenty of visitors.

You see, since the cemetery opened in 1848, it has been plagued with reports of the ghosts of monks, lovers, children, and even Jose Cuervo. There were also reports of a vampire using the cemetery as his lair.

But the creepiest of all the stories associated with the cemetery have to do with a boy called Nachito.

According to the legend, Nachito was so afraid of the dark that he could only sleep at night with two lit torches outside his bedroom window (this was the late 1800s). Well, one night a storm blew the torches out and little Nachito was found by his parents the next morning, dead from an apparent heart attack. Nachito was promptly buried in the cemetery. But his coffin was discovered aboveground the next morning, next to the hole where it should have been. The townspeople buried Nachito once more, but he miraculously rose to the surface again. This happened a total of nine times.

Finally, Nachito's family interred him in an aboveground crypt where he would be exposed to the sunlight.

The mysterious risings of Nachito stopped. However, due to the apparently otherworldly aspect of this situation—combined with all of the other ghost sightings—the cemetery closed.

If you're a brave soul, though, you can still go there at night to see if you can spot Nachito or one of the other apparitions said to frequent the cemetery.

Jose Cuervo Was a Real Person

No doubt, you're familiar with the tequila Jose Cuervo. We discussed it little bit in the previous chapter—it was a company started by the Cuervo family in the town of Tequila, Jalisco. There are some popular misconceptions about Jose Cuervo, though. Did he exist, or didn't he? Some people think that he is just a marketing gimmick thought up by the company. Not so. Jose Cuervo was a real man.

Don Jose Antonio de Cuervo was born in Spain. But when opportunities for advancement dried up, he made his way across the Atlantic to New Spain. He was given a land grant by King Ferdinand VII of Spain, and shortly thereafter he began using the agave plant to make tequila.

By all accounts, he died a wealthy and happy man. Even so, some say his ghost still walks the site of the original distillery. Others say they can find him at the Santa Paula Cemetery.

I guess you'll have to check it out for yourself—the drink and the ghost stories!

The Origins of the Margarita Remain Unknown

The margarita is thought to be the quintessential Mexican mixed drink. The main ingredient is tequila, which is mixed with orange liqueur and lime juice. While tequila is certainly a Mexican alcohol, details regarding the margarita's first appearance remains open to debate.

The most popular story is that Mexican bar owner Danny Herrera first mixed the drink in 1938 at his rural Baja California bar. He prepared it for a regular American customer who was allergic to most distilled alcohols. One of Herrera's bartenders later brought the drink recipe with him north of the border in the 1940s, and the rest is history.

But not all agree.

Texas socialite Margarita Sames claims to have invented the drink while vacationing in Acapulco in 1948. The name certainly sounds right, but historians are generally in agreement that the drink was already around by the late 1930s.

Many people defer to what they believe is the authority in this matter: the Jose Cuervo Company.

The company stated in the 1940s that the drink was invented by a bartender in the 1930s for a woman he was in love with named Rita de la Rosa. Her name wasn't Margarita, but most people go with the originators of tequila on this one.

The mysterious origins of the margarita may never be solved, but it sure is fun to talk about when you're having a few.

Demon Dogs

If you ever visit some of the villages in Chiapas or Campeche and have a few cervezas, you might want to ask about *el Cadejo*. Or maybe not. You see Cadejo is the name of a supernatural animal that many people in the region that borders Guatemala swear exists.

They also swear it can kill people.

Based on supposed eyewitness descriptions, Cadejo can best be described as a dog-goat hybrid. It looks primarily like a dog, but instead of paws it has creepy devil-like hooves. The color of these creatures differs and can determine—if you're unfortunate enough to encounter one—whether you'll live or die. Black Cadejos are said to be evil and extremely powerful, while white Cadejos act as protectors of nighttime travelers.

Cadejos have been sighted in southern Mexico, Guatemala, and El Salvador for more than one hundred years. But as of today, none have yet been captured.

If you see one, you should quickly go the other way. It is said that few people who have encountered a Cadejo have survived, and those who have, have been left with permanent physical and psychological damage.

The Goat Suckers

Another mythical canine beast sometimes associated with Mexico is the chupacabra. The name means "goat sucker"; whenever one of these creatures has been spotted in a rural area, it leaves dead farm animals—sucked dry of their blood—in its wake.

The story of the chupacabra begins in the remote areas of the Puerto Rican highlands in 1995. It was during that year when farmers began finding their prized goats dead, drained of all blood. The only evidence that pointed toward anything were two puncture marks left on the animals' necks.

The chupacabra was described as a bipedal creature, about four to five feet tall, with scaly skin, a head that resembles that of a "gray alien," and long, claw-like fingers. Numerous sightings of the scary creature were reported around Puerto Rico and other Latin American countries throughout the 1990s.

By the time sightings of these creatures made it to Mexico in the late 1990s, it had evolved into a medium-sized hairless canine creature. The sightings of these strange creatures were especially prevalent along the northern border with the United States. Finally, by the late 2000s, chupacabra corpses began to materialize in Texas. These remains could be professionally tested in labs. All of the tests revealed that the chupacabras were either domestic dogs, coyotes, wolves, or a mixture of the three. Experts believe that the bizarre appearance of these creatures is primarily the result of mange or other infections.

But not everyone in Mexico is convinced.

Some think that it is some new type of hybrid animal, while other think it is more otherworldly, a variation or some type of relative of El Cadejo.

RANDOM FACTS

1. On the border of the state of Puebla and Mexico are two large volcanic mountains named Popocatépetl and Iztaccíhuatl. According to legend, Popocatépetl was once a mighty Aztec warrior who wanted to marry Iztaccíhuatl, but a rival suitor told the young woman that her warrior boyfriend died in battle. Iztaccíhuatl then died of heartbreak, and when Popocatépetl returned he had her interred on top of the mountain. Afterwards, he transformed into a mountain and they now spend eternity together.

2. Pan de muerto, "bread of the dead," is one of the primary foods associated with Day of the Dead celebrations. It is a traditional Mexican sweetbread.

3. There is another story of a haunted house in Monterrey. It doesn't really look like a haunted house. It is actually a post-modern design that looks like a bunch of concrete cylinders or tubes, which is why it is called "the house of tubes." The original owner's paralyzed daughter died in the house before it was completed, as did a couple of workers. Then, when a new couple moved into the house and their son died, the local authorities closed it down. Some brave

souls occasionally enter the boarded-up house to see the ghost of the paralyzed girl.

4. The first known publication of a drink that uses the same ingredients as a margarita was in the 1937 *Café Royal Cocktail Book*, but it wasn't called a margarita. The first known publication that referred to the drink as a margarita was a 1953 issue of *Esquire* magazine.

5. It is believed that the blindfolding of the person hitting the piñata was originally a Mayan element of the tradition.

6. A bizarre Mexican serial killer legend involves the house of the Counts of la Torre Cosío y la Cortina in central Mexico City. It is believed that the home's owner, González de Cossio, believed he was being cuckolded by his wife, so he summoned a mystic who told him to kill the first man who passed by at 11:00 pm. Cossio did this, and he liked killing so much that he kept on doing it. Later, he mysteriously died while asking for penance.

7. The lake that surrounded the Island of Aztlan was called Metzliapan or "Lake of the Moon."

8. The Chihuahua dog has a short- and a long-haired variety. It is believed that the short-haired variety physically resembles its ancient ancestor more than the long-haired type.

9. Pope Leo XIII gave the image of the Virgin of Guadalupe a Canonical Coronation on October 12, 1895.

10. Due to the creepy story and the number of reported encounters, the house at 1026 Jose Aramberri Street in Monterrey has attracted numerous parapsychologists over the years. None, however, have been able to capture much on camera.

11. Men around the world are concerned about hair loss and receding hairlines, right? Well, one superstition in Mexico says that if you rub a special concoction that includes chicken poop as the key ingredient, your hair will grow back!

12. If you travel through the mountainous regions of Mexico, you might hear about Las Ciguapas. They are like a combination of a siren and a succubus, as they seduce men, take their energy, and them kill them.

13. One strange pseudo-science myth prevalent in Mexico is that if you hang bags of water from your ceiling they will repel flies. The origins of this myth are unknown, but it is quite poplar in some of the poorer and more rural areas of the country.

14. In the United States, we have the Bogeyman, but in Mexico he is called *El Cuco*. Basically, El Cuco

is the same as the Bogeyman: He hides under children's beds and eats the ones who are bad.

15. The Aztecs believed in fairy or sprite-like creatures, known as *chaneques*, that inhabited the forests. The Aztecs believe these to be malevolent creatures. After Catholicism became the religion of the land, belief in them persisted; it was thought that they were the souls of unbaptized children.

16. There has been a revival of interest in Aztec and Mayan culture in recent years from some unlikely sources. New Age types have created what they believe are authentic Aztec and Mayan rituals (minus the human sacrifice), and Mexican-American gangs often employ Aztec imagery as part of their style, even using the Nahuatl language to send secret messages.

17. One common Mexican superstition is that pregnant women shouldn't go outside during an eclipse, and if they do, they need to place a safety pin on their belly. The superstition has its origin in Aztec culture.

18. If you're traveling through Mexico, you may notice that women rarely place their purses on the floor. It isn't necessarily due to sanitary reasons; it's more because they believe that doing so will lead to one losing their money.

19. In 2012, a U.S. federal judge in New Mexico ruled that paraphernalia of Jesus Malverde could be used by the prosecution in a drug smuggling case. It was perhaps the first time in history where a person's patronage of a "saint" was used against him.

20. There are some strange legends and superstitions concerning pimples in Mexico. One states that if you point at a rainbow you'll get a zit on your nose, while another holds that if you watch a dog take a dump you'll get one on your eye.

Test Yourself – Questions

1. This man was the original narco saint:

   a. Jesus Malverde
   b. Juan Valverde
   c. Pablo Escobar

2. The mythical homeland of the Aztecs was called:

   a. Atlantis
   b. Hyperborea
   c. Aztlan

3. Mexicans often dress up like skeletons on which holiday?

   a. Halloween
   b. Day of the Dead
   c. Lent

4. These otherworldly creatures resemble dogs with hoofs:

   a. Cadejos
   b. Bigfoots
   c. Hombres

5. What is often referred to as the most haunted cemetery in Mexico?

   a. Santa Paula Cemetery
   b. San Juan Cemetery
   c. El Crypt Keeper's Casa

Answers

1. a
2. c
3. b
4. a
5. a

DON'T FORGET YOUR
FREE BOOKS

GET THEM FOR FREE ON
WWW.TRIVIABILL.COM

MORE BOOKS YOU MIGHT LIKE

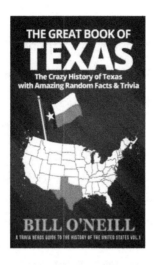

Are you looking to learn more about Texas? Sure, you've heard about the Alamo and JFK's assassination in history class, but there's so much about the Lone Star State that even natives don't know about. In this trivia book, you'll journey through Texas's history, pop culture, sports, folklore, and so much more!

In *The Great Book of Texas*, some of the things you will learn include:

- Which Texas hero isn't even from Texas?
- Why is Texas called the Lone Star State?
- Which hotel in Austin is one of the most haunted hotels in the United States?

- Where was Bonnie and Clyde's hideout located?
- Which Tejano musician is buried in Corpus Christi?

What unsolved mysteries happened in the state?

Which Texas-born celebrity was voted "Most Handsome" in high school?

Which popular TV show star just opened a brewery in Austin?

You'll find out the answers to these questions and learn many other facts. Some of them will be fun, some of them will creepy, and some of them will be sad, but all of them will be fascinating! This book is jam-packed with everything you could have ever wondered about Texas.

Whether you consider yourself a Texas pro, or you know absolutely nothing about the state, you'll learn something new as you discover more about the state's past, present, and future. Find out about things that weren't mentioned in your history book. In fact, once you've finished reading, you might even be able to impress your history teacher with your newfound knowledge! So, what are you waiting for? Dive in now to learn all there is to know about the Lone Star State!

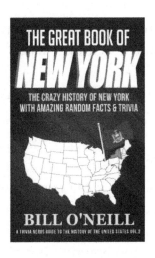

THE GREAT BOOK OF

NEW YORK

THE CRAZY HISTORY OF NEW YORK
WITH AMAZING RANDOM FACTS & TRIVIA

BILL O'NEILL

A TRIVIA NERDS GUIDE TO THE HISTORY OF THE UNITED STATES VOL. 2

Want to learn more about New York? Sure, you've heard about the Statue of Liberty, but how much do you really know about the Empire State? Do you know why it's even called the Empire State? There's so much about New York that even the natives don't know. In this trivia book, you'll learn about New York's history, pop culture, folklore, sports, and so much more!

In *The Great Book of New York*, you'll learn the answers to the following questions:

- Why is New York City called the Big Apple?
- What genre of music started out in New York City?
- Which late actress's life is celebrated at a festival held in her hometown every year?
- Which monster might be living in a lake in New York?

- Was there really a Staten Island bogeyman?
- Which movie is loosely based on New York in the 1800s?
- Which cult favorite cake recipe got its start in New York?
- Why do the New York Yankees have pinstripe uniforms?

These are just a few of the many facts you'll find in this book. Some of them will be fun, some of them will be sad, and some of them will be so chilling they'll give you goosebumps, but all of them will be fascinating! This book is full of everything you've ever wondered about New York.

It doesn't matter if you consider yourself an expert of New York, or if you know nothing about the Empire State. You're bound to learn something new as you journey through each chapter. You'll be able to impress your friends on your next trivia night!

So, what are you waiting for? Dive in now so you can learn all there is to know about New York!

Are you interested in learning more about California? Sure, you've heard of Hollywood, but how much do you really know about the Golden State? Do you know how it got its nickname or what it was nicknamed first? There's so much to know about California that even people born in the state don't know it all. In this trivia book, you'll learn about California's history, pop culture, folklore, sports, and so much more!

In *The Great Book of California*, you'll discover the answers to the following questions

- Why is California called the Golden State?
- What music genres started out in California?
- Which celebrity sex icon's death remains a mystery?
- Which serial killer once murdered in the state?

- Which childhood toy started out in California?
- Which famous fast-food chain opened its first location in the Golden State?
- Which famous athletes are from California?

These are just a few of the many facts you'll find in this book. Some of them will be entertaining, some of them will be tragic, and some of them may haunt you, but all of them will be interesting! This book is full of everything you've ever wondered about California and then some!

Whether you consider yourself an expert of California, or you know nothing at all about the Golden State, you're bound to learn something new in each chapter. You'll be able to impress your college history professor or your friends during your next trivia night!

What are you waiting for? Get started learning all there is to know about California.

MORE BOOKS BY BILL O'NEILL

I hope you enjoyed this book and learned something new. Please feel free to check out some of my previous books on Amazon.

Made in the USA
Las Vegas, NV
26 April 2023